Contents

List of Boxes

List of Tables

Acknowledgments

Gillian Pugh, then director of the National Children's Bureau's Early Childhood Unit, was the original inspiration for this project – as with so many other initiatives that have furthered the cause of young children and their parents. Without her impeccable management, advice and support the book would never have been finished. Nor would it have started without the essential financial support for the project provided by Paul Curno of the Calouste Gulbenkian Foundation.

Chris Catanach, Trevor Chandler, Bernadette Duffy, Sue Emerson, Anne Grose-Hodge, Siri Heaven, Sue Reynolds, Jeannette Scholes, Janette Smith, Sheila Thorpe, and Eileen Torbet were very generous indeed with their time and support, as were all their colleagues, and other professionals involved in the work of the centres. The perceptions and comments of all the parents I talked to were also very helpful indeed.

At a time when too many of those involved in education feel ground-down and depressed, it was a great pleasure and privilege to visit establishments with such highly motivated and successful professionals, such enthusiastic and grateful parents, and such confident and cheerful children.

The author

Virginia Makins worked for the *Sunday Telegraph* and *The Observer* before specialising in education journalism and moving to *The Times Educational Supplement* in 1969. At the *TES* she was Features Editor and Deputy Editor, and after the birth of her three children, continued on the paper part-time as a writer and editor. She is the author of *The Invincible Children: Nipping failure in the bud* (David Fulton, 1997).

Foreword

Father: 'But it's only a nursery.'
Mother: 'It's not just a nursery. It's our life.'

Anyone visiting the United Kingdom and trying to understand the complex but uncoordinated range of services available to young children before they start formal schooling would be forgiven for saying that they wouldn't have started from here. Despite the very obvious fact that young children and their families have a wide range of needs which cannot be neatly divided into 'care' or 'education' or 'play' for children, or 'advice' or 'training' or 'support' for their parents, there are still remarkably few multi-agency centres such as those described in this book, and still fewer primary schools that have broadened their early years work in this way.

In the 25 years since the first centre opened at Hillfields in Coventry, countless reports have pointed to the lack of coordination between services and the shortfall between what is available and what families are asking for. They have recommended integration at central and local government level and in the provision of local services. And yet the historical divisions, the professional jealousies, and the barriers created by different priorities, philosophies and training have made for very slow progress.

In this book Virginia Makins looks at ten centres that have succeeded, often against considerable odds, in providing a more complete and coherent service for families in their locality. Some are purpose built, some are linked to schools, others started with the opportunist conversion of an empty building. Some are one-off examples, others are part of a network across a local authority. But they all share several key characteristics. They are open to all families, not just to those who are referred by social and health services. They work in close partnership with parents, and across agencies. They provide informal professional support to parents, in a way that is readily accepted. They emphasise children's learning and the development of an appropriate curriculum, often not just for children of normal nursery age, but for babies and toddlers. They 'reach out' into the community to those who do not readily use services. Many of the centres also offer a range of education and training opportunities for parents and other adults. They have leaders with vision, who put a high priority on staff development and training.

We sought funding to write this book because of our continuing belief that this is the way in which services for young children should develop. There is widespread agreement across all sectors, and evidence from centres such as those in our study, that such services can bring considerable benefits to parents and children, particularly in areas of high need. We hope that this book will provide both the example and the inspiration that policy makers, managers and practitioners need if growth over the next 25 years is to be more impressive.

Gillian Pugh
Director, Early Childhood Unit, National Children's Bureau

1. Long road to integration

The benefits of working together

The first combined nursery centre opened in Hillfields in inner Coventry in 1971. The aim was to provide a flexible and accessible service for all the parents and young children in one neighbourhood, breaking down the barriers that had grown up between education, social services and health services. It was an idea whose time seemed to have come, and a few similar centres soon opened in other areas.

The benefits of different services working together in neighbourhood centres were, and still are, evident. They include:

- meeting young children's needs as a whole: care, education and health are interdependent;
- providing flexible services as parents need them;
- preventing gaps and overlaps in services provided by different agencies;
- making the best use of resources;
- giving all families support as and when they need it: minimising unproductive labelling and stigma;
- improving assessment of 'need';
- promoting quality educational opportunities for children from a very early age, and involving their parents;
- relieving the stress of coping with young children for those living in poverty, and poor housing conditions;
- sharing the various skills and expertise of different professionals, and providing multi-disciplinary staff development and training to help them meet the needs of young children;
- helping to ensure that all services aspire to high quality standards.

In the 25 years since Hillfields opened, the potential of multi-agency early years centres is more evident than ever, with many examples of successful practice.

Three separate services

However, in spite of years of exhortation that services must work together, in many places barriers between social services, which are responsible for day care for young children and for services for children in need, education authorities, which run nursery schools and classes, and community health services, which support parents of young children and monitor children's physical development, are still entrenched at every level. (For a fuller account of the history of the separate development of education and care services see Ferri and others, 1981.)

Nursery education

Nursery education developed as a system of part-time sessions for three- and four-year-olds during school terms, mainly in classes attached to primary schools. Provision of state nursery places is sparse or non-existent outside large cities. The voluntary playgroup movement that grew up to fill the gap generally offers children two or three low-cost part-time sessions each week. State nursery education has high status with parents, and schools and classes are open to all comers meeting the schools' entry criteria. They are staffed by trained teachers. But part-time places in term-time are little help to working parents, or to parents living stressful lives at the bottom of the social and economic ladder.

When the birth-rate declined sharply in the 1970s, creating extra space in primary schools, many local authorities responded to the shortage of nursery places by bringing younger four-year-olds into reception classes of primary schools rather than starting new nursery classes. Often few or no extra resources or staff training was provided to make sure that the schools adapted to the needs of very young children.

Day care

Since the second world war, public sector day care has mainly become a restricted service for families and children 'at risk' or in acute difficulties. It is run by social services departments, and tight 'priority' criteria restrict access to places. So state day nurseries have been linked with considerable stigma and sometimes dissatisfaction. In 1976, one researcher found that 'unlike nursery school staff, who are convinced of the positive value of their work, day nursery staff have no great confidence in theirs. And the gloom is a breeding ground for a faulty service.' (Boyle, 1976).

Day nurseries are mainly staffed by nursery nurses, many of them 16-year-old school leavers with a two-year training focused on the day-to-day care of young children in normal circumstance. There is little or no preparation to work with parents in very difficult circumstances. The lack of public provision has led to a big growth of private sector day care for better-off working parents, and to the widespread use of childminders looking after children in their homes.

Some social workers became dissatisfied with state provision that simply cared for the neediest children for a few hours a day. One response was to switch the emphasis from day care to 'family centres' where social work professionals worked with parents and children together, trying to improve parenting skills. Local social services departments and voluntary bodies set up many such centres, and the Children Act of 1989 encouraged their development.

These centres often have to work with reluctant and angry clients, who feel they are forced to attend if they want to avoid their children being taken into care. There can be considerable stigma attached to referral. Moreover, in places where family centres and day care have been opened up to all parents in a neighbourhood there are always some 'ordinary' children and families who turn out to have difficulties as great, or greater, than the families who have been identified as 'in need' and referred for support. (For example, see Whalley, 1994, Statham, 1994 and Smith, 1996.)

Community health services

In theory, community health services should reach all children and families. Health visitors visit all parents of new-born babies, and run clinics to monitor children's development and provide parents with advice and support. Those with special needs should be referred on to appropriate professionals, such as speech and physiotherapists. But the child health services can be patchy, depending on the energy and confidence of individual health professionals. Parents living under the greatest stress find it most difficult to make use of clinics and regular health checks.

Parents

For many years, the national debate about provision for under fives focused on children – the shortage of day care and nursery places, and the importance of early education and preventive child health programmes. But increasingly, professionals and researchers into early childhood development began to see that meeting *parents*' needs, and supporting them as the prime carers and educators of their young children, was crucial to children's healthy and happy development.

A number of projects were started to support parents, and in some cases more overtly to educate them about their children's needs. Some nursery and primary schools began to welcome parents on to the premises, providing parents' rooms and groups. The Open University and other organisations provided useful materials for such groups to work with. Voluntary organisations were started to help educate and support parents – though they did not have the resources to reach the parents in most need of support.

A few local authorities, such as Hampshire and Manchester, have set out to provide an authority-wide network of centres with the aim of supporting parents of young children. But many schemes to support parents have been one-off ventures, depending on the energy of individual professionals or voluntary organisations. (See Pugh and others, 1994, for a full account of policies and practice for parent education and support.)

Combined nursery centres – one stop shops for parents

Hillfields combined nursery centre in Coventry was set up in the belief that better coordination between services would be achieved by putting services under one roof. Other pioneer centres soon followed: by 1975, there were seven of them. They were all in 'social priority' areas, and they set out to offer a flexible mix of nursery education, day care and advice and support for parents.

The centres rapidly stumbled over the barriers they were intended to remove. At the grass roots there were much-publicised problems when teachers and nursery nurses, with their different status and very different pay and conditions of service, came together under one roof. The teachers were better paid, and had longer holidays – but it often seemed to the nursery nurses that they were all doing much the same job. There were also continuing anomalies that puzzled or infuriated parents. Nursery education places were free, whereas there were sometimes charges for the day care places, even though those places were often still restricted to children 'at risk'.

At the local authority level, education and social services departments found it difficult to work together and offer integrated management and support to the centres. (The health contribution was generally simpler, providing health professionals to run clinics and groups within a centre.) There was no material support for coordination at national level, only exhortations from the Department of Education and Science and the Department of Health and Social Security (DHSS/DES 1976 and 1978). The two government departments did also jointly fund a three-year research project into the existing joint centres, which started in 1975 (Ferri and others, 1981).

The research team studied four of the seven existing centres. It found that the children in the new centres did just as well as children in separate nursery schools and day nurseries. But none of the centres had managed to eradicate the divisions between social services priority day care and open access nursery education. 'The four centres in no way represented a form of nursery provision which was based on consumer choice', the research team concluded.

They found staff reluctant to encourage the participation of parents – particularly the 'priority' day care parents – in the work of the nursery. 'Education' services did not always reach the younger children in the day nursery. Local authority administrative structures perpetuated the old divisions. The centres' leaders were not well supported by council officers in their attempts to make a reality of the original aims.

But it was very early days. The vision of integrated centres that could work flexibly to meet the individual needs of children and families, and ensure that services worked together, survived, and the number of combined centres continued to grow slowly, building on the experience of the pioneers. A survey of services for children under five in all local authorities in England, Scotland and Wales, undertaken by the National Children's Bureau in 1986, found 22 combined nursery centres, and 20 extended-day schemes in schools (Pugh, 1988).

At that time eight local authorities were planning new combined centres and four were about to start new extended day schemes in schools, mainly in city areas. 45 other local authorities had plans for other services for children under five and their parents, such as open access family centres offering support and educational opportunities for children with their parents, rather than full scale nursery education and day care.

A few local authorities, led by Strathclyde in 1986, tried to tackle the structural barriers between services by integrating care and education within one department. Strathclyde made the education department responsible for all services for pre-school children, and a few other local authorities, such as Sheffield and Kirklees and several inner London boroughs, followed suit. Manchester set up a Children's Services department to oversee early years care and education. Other authorities tried to integrate services for young children by setting up joint sub-committees of their education and social services departments.

But even in these authorities, research for the Audit Commission showed that outside forces such as budget cuts, or new statutory requirements on the different services, made it very difficult to plan rationally across service divides (Pugh and McQuail, 1995).

Blocks to development

The blocks and barriers to setting up joint services still remain. They include:

- different legislation (successive Education Acts, Health legislation, the Children Act for social services);
- different professional values and priorities;
- different geographical and statutory boundaries;
- different training;

- different levels of status and authority;
- different management styles;
- different pay and conditions of service;
- mutual distrust between services.

The Children Act and the 1990s

The far-reaching provisions of the 1989 Children Act did promote and highlight coordination between the different authorities dealing with children 'in need'.[1] The Act emphasised the importance of prevention, and of open-access neighbourhood services for families.

It requires local authority education and social services departments jointly to review the level, pattern and range of day care and related services. They have to consult local health authorities, the voluntary sector, minority groups, employer and parent interests and other interested bodies. Such reviews have to take place every three years, and the reports have to be published. Information about 'centres of excellence', training opportunities, and the range of support services for families have to be included in the report. However, the review does not cover nursery education, apart from providing information about its quantity and availability.

Cuts in social services budgets, and other pressures, have meant that the preventive aspects of the Children Act have in practice been swamped by the extensive regulations and requirements for child protection. A major 1994 Audit Commission report on services for children (covering health and social services but not education) found that 'field social workers appear to have insufficient time to undertake more proactive work in support of children in need – particularly because of the pressures of child protection work.' (Audit Commission 1994, p 9.)

The Department of Health has also promoted better coordination between services. *The Health of the Nation* called for 'healthy alliances' – active partnerships between agencies to promote health targets, and subsequent guidance has stressed the importance of coordination in services for children (DH, 1992). But the radical changes in the National Health Service, imposing a split between 'purchasers' and 'providers', and introducing new contracts for general practitioners, have if anything increased the fragmentation of community health services.

Many GPs have taken over responsibility for community child health within their practice, employing their own health visitors. So the health

---

1   In the Guidance to the Children Act (HMSO 1990) 'in need' is defined as children who are 'unlikely to achieve or maintain, or to have the opportunity of achieving and maintaining, a reasonable standard of health and development without the provision...of services by a local authority', as well as disabled children and children whose health or development is likely to be 'significantly impaired' without the provision of services

visitors no longer cover a particular local area, but instead are responsible only for the patients in their own GP practice. This has made regular cooperation with other services on a neighbourhood basis more difficult.

Reporting on community child health in its 1994 report, the Audit Commission found poor information and management, and 'a lack of clarity over service objectives and outcomes, with insufficient collaboration between professionals'. (Audit Commission, 1994, p.8.) They recommended that services should be better targeted to children and families that need most help – further weakening the idea of a universal child health service.

But one of the report's general conclusions was that:

> Authorities and professionals must work together to plan and deliver services. Family support should be provided jointly, and be given a higher priority. It should make the most of the different skills of people working in health and voluntary agencies, social services and educational authorities, and parents working as volunteers in the community. At present there is little joint agreement on needs and service planning...With responsibility for services increasingly shared between agencies, and the provision of services increasingly fragmenting, the likelihood of gaps and duplication will grow unless effective joint action is taken. (Audit Commission 1994 p.1)

Meanwhile the national debate about nursery education continued to be about the availability, quantity and quality of part-time provision for three- and four-year-olds, with little concern about younger children, all- day care, or support for their parents. *Starting with Quality*, the report of the Rumbold committee (DES 1990) focused on the education of three- and four-year-olds, and quality issues such as evaluation and training within the conventional part-time nursery framework (DES 1990).

Reports by non-government organisations such as the National Commission for Education (NCE 1993) and the Royal Society of Arts (Ball 1994) highlighted the crucial importance of nursery education, and called for the expansion of publicly-funded provision along traditional lines. This narrow focus looked to be narrowed further by the scheme for nursery vouchers, introduced in four pilot areas in 1996 and due to go national in 1997. All parents of four-year-olds are to be given vouchers worth £1100 to spend on five part-time sessions a week of education in any institution approved by a short inspection. A more promising scenario is offered by the Labour party document, *Early Excellence*, which promotes the concept of multi-agency centres (see final chapter).

Multi-agency neighbourhood centres: ten case studies

In spite of all the pressures on services in the 1990s, and the overall context of fragmentation outlined above, multi-agency early years centres have remained an aspiration for many, and the number of centres jointly funded by different agencies has slowly grown. In 1996, the National Children's Bureau, in an attempt to encourage this growth, secured funding from the Gulbenkian Foundation for a set of ten case studies, to disseminate information about the centres' aims and practice, the services they offered, and how they were overcoming the blocks to inter-agency cooperation.

The Bureau's Early Childhood Unit wrote to all local authorities in England, and to its sister organisations Children in Wales and Children in Scotland, as well as to all the main national childcare organisations, asking them to suggest suitable examples of multi-agency early years centres for the study. They were sent information on 110 centres in 57 local authorities. This is no guide to the number of centres now in existence. Many local authorities did not reply, and others sent one or two examples chosen from several in their area.

A number of centres had been mainly or partly funded by the voluntary sector: there were examples of centres run in partnership with the NSPCC, NCH Action for Children, Barnados, Save the Children, and the Church Diocesan Board. Some local authorities only had one centre. Others had a whole network. Gloucestershire had 15, Salford had ten, Manchester had six (and has since developed more centres based in primary schools). Two authorities were planning to set up centres in the near future.

Hampshire was well on the way to developing centres in every district of the county, building them on to a range of existing services – schools, social services family centres, voluntary-run centres. Cambridgeshire had no local authority centres, but has helped to build a network of centres run by other agencies.

Some of the centres, both long-standing and relatively new ones, had been purpose built. Others were created by extending existing nursery schools, or combining them with day nurseries or family centres. We were sent only one example of a centre based in a further education college, in Bridgewater in Somerset, but there are others. We had hoped for examples of multi-agency work based in primary schools, since that seemed the most hopeful route for spreading the work more widely, but the very few that came in were still in their infancy and not suitable for this study.

We were also sent interesting examples of multi-agency training initiatives. The London Borough of Haringey, in cooperation with neighbouring Enfield, has set up a Childcare, Education and Training network, involving the Training and Employment Council and local colleges and the voluntary sector, which has recently attracted funding from the Single Regeneration Budget.

Selecting ten centres from this great range of provision was not easy. We made no attempt to identify the 'ten best' centres. Instead, the final list was chosen to show something of the *variety* of multi-agency centres, and of their funding and management arrangements. We had to leave out some outstanding examples of good practice. We included two examples of authority-wide approaches to supporting families with young children, in Hampshire and Gloucestershire. But we had to leave out others that have developed significant provision, such as Salford and the London Borough of Islington.

In particular, we would have liked to include a centre in Manchester, which has several children's centres, planned and opened since 1986, but in the event the city council did not wish us to include a case study of one of their centres. When many centres have moved away from providing full five day a week care for parents who are working or studying, Manchester built some centres around open access day care, with extra space for community use and other services such as playgroups and after school care.

We reluctantly left out the Riverside Early Years Training Centre, a new flagship City Challenge project in North Tyneside. It is an ambitious venture, partly funded by the European Social Fund, and it includes two nurseries, an after school club, and extensive training facilities. But its unusually generous funding will make it difficult to replicate. We also left out an interesting centre in the middle of the West End of London: the Soho Family Centre. It works with many families of Chinese and Bengali origin, and provides a base for childminders in an area where houses and flats are not very suitable for caring for children.

The final selection of ten centres covers a very wide range. Some provide extensive services, others quite limited ones. They differ in their origins; the areas they serve – inner city, urban, rural – their resources and staffing; and their objectives. Seven of the centres in the study either fit the full-blown concept of combined multi-agency, flexible provision to meet the needs of local families, or come close to it. They are:

Hillfields Nursery Centre, Coventry. Hillfields opened in 1971 as the first post-war centre combining day care and education. As jobs became increasingly scarce, it developed more flexible provision with facilities for parents and young children, and sessions for care and education for children under three, some of whom can stay all day, and for three- to five-year-olds. It is open all year, and provides opportunities and groups for adults as well as children.

The Pen Green Centre, Corby. Pen Green has featured in government and research reports, and become a model, nationally and internationally. It offers year-round nursery education, with full- and part-time places for two- to five-year-olds, playgroups, extensive education, training and support groups for adults (including some closed therapeutic groups). Social work and health professionals are directly involved in providing its services.

Greengables, Edinburgh. Greengables has grown from a nursery school to a multi-purpose family centre in a few years, helped by an Urban Aid grant which provided a new building for adult groups and community ventures. It offers education and extended day care for under fives, parent support, adult education, holiday play schemes and other community services. Its staff includes a social worker, a home-visiting teacher, and a community education specialist.

Netherton Family Centre, Dudley is another nursery school that has grown to meet the needs of local families. In 1995, with funding from the local council and from NCH Action for Children, it moved into a new building, purpose-designed for integrating family support and adult education with the work of the nursery school. It provides some all-day care, after school and holiday care, integrated support for children with special needs, adult groups, and services for under threes and their parents.

The Dorothy Gardner Centre, London was one of the first combined centres, built to serve a small, mixed, cosmopolitan neighbourhood in North Westminster. It provides day care and education for children from two to five, an open drop-in for parents with young children, and a range of adult groups. It sees its 'core business' as the education of children from babyhood to five, and, with five specialist nursery teachers on the staff, it has been a powerful force for early years curriculum development, in partnership with parents.

The Patmore Centre, London. Save the Children started this centre in a flat on a housing estate in Wandsworth. It was so successful that the charity designed a purpose-built centre to expand the work. At the time of writing, it provided a day nursery, adult education and training, and an advice and advocacy service for adults, and it has promoted several local community development projects and initiatives in parent support, literacy, and child care training.

The Sandal Agbrigg Pre-fives Centre, Wakefield was built five years ago to offer day care, nursery education and support to local families. Two years later it shut its semi-separate day nursery so its staff could concentrate on family support, but it offers some all day places and respite care. Its permanent staff includes social workers as well as teachers.

Two of the centres are examples of strong local authority policies to provide a network of neighbourhood centres to support families with young children. They are:

Robinswood Family Centre, Gloucester. Robinswood has limited staffing and resources of its own. But with energetic leadership, and good partnerships with its host primary school and other local agencies, it has developed an extensive range of services for parents and children, including part-time nursery education (but no day care), support for parents with babies and young children, and adult education.

The Chase Children's Centre, Hampshire. The Chase is the oldest of Hampshire's network of centres. Its new building was provided by local fund-raising, and its recurrent funding comes from the education and social services departments and the local health trust. It runs sessions for parents with their children under five, and has a particular focus on early support for children with special needs and their parents. It also helps to run some outreach groups.

Finally, there is an example of a new centre set up to serve a rural area.

The ACE Centre, Chipping Norton started when two primary schools were merged, leaving a separate nursery school adjoining an otherwise empty school building. The centre was funded jointly by Oxfordshire County Council Education and Social Services Departments, and by the Rural Development Commission. As well as the nursery school, it includes an open-access social services family centre, a computer training centre, after-school and holiday care, and some community education.

The case studies are based on two day visits to the centres, and interviews with local professionals familiar with their work.

The visits focused particularly on:

- the context of the centre's work: the nature of the local area; local authority policies; funding and management;
- services for children, and for parents as parents;
- services for adults and the community;
- quality issues: professional training and development; curriculum review and development; assessment and recording children's progress; equal opportunities;
- work with children with special needs;
- admission policies;
- partnership with parents: parent involvement and empowerment;
- multi-agency working: links with other local professionals and services for them, benefits, difficulties;
- funding, staffing and management;
- what workers saw as distinctive and special about their work, and the frustrations they encountered.

The case studies are descriptive reports, not critical evaluations. The aim is to show what is happening, and what is possible, even in the present climate when funding is very tight and there are intense pressures and demands on all three contributing services.

Several common threads emerge from the case studies. When an institution is working across professional boundaries, with staff from different backgrounds and training, leadership is even more crucial than usual. Leaders often have to work in some isolation: their work does not fit into the usual administrative categories and support systems.

Staff training and development is perhaps the most important task of the leaders. Centres that have negotiated reasonable non-contact time for training, review and record keeping have a built-in advantage when it comes to quality and service development.

There had been a great deal of recent curriculum review and reorganisation. The trend was to give children more choice and autonomy, within a scaffolding of careful observation and recording of their activities and progress. Some centres had undertaken interesting and productive curriculum development for babies and toddlers,

Several centres were losing four-year-olds to primary school reception classes, even though their nurseries were very popular, and could offer more flexible services to parents than the schools. Parents felt under pressure to send children to their chosen primary school early to ensure a place. Nursery vouchers would be likely to increase the competition.

More than one centre had recently had to cut back services because of cuts in their funding, and senior staff were spending increasing amounts of time fund-raising. One centre (Patmore) was facing the possibility of having to close its core day nursery service altogether. The centres were seen as expensive, partly because those unfamiliar with the range of their work compared them with straight nursery classes, day nurseries or family centres.

These issues are discussed in more detail in the final chapter.

Table 2.1   Hillfields Nursery Centre

Services for children and parents	Opportunities for parents	Links with other professionals	Funding and management
Sessions for parents and children from birth upwards.	Support and advice for parents at any time.	Link meeting with health visitor and doctor every week.	Grant of £462,000 from education and social services. Education department responsible for the centre.
Nursery for two to three-year-olds, offering flexible allocation of half- day and all-day sessions.	Cookery and social groups.	Close partnership with social workers over families in need.	Delegated budget.
Nursery for three and four-year-olds, generally offering two all-day sessions a week.	Ad hoc groups to help with parenting problems, when wanted.	Centre used for contact visits and case conferences.	Some funds raised from other bodies and local donors.
Centre open all year round.	Variety of speakers invited in.	Family workers take part in assessments.	Management committee with parent, staff, community and council representatives. No executive responsibility for the budget.
Bilingual assistants speaking Asian community languages.	Accredited access courses building skills and confidence for further education.		
Creche.			
Doctor visits monthly.			
Speech therapist visits every six weeks.			

2. Hillfields Nursery Centre, Coventry

Introduction

Hillfields, in Coventry, is an area of utilitarian inner city post-war re-development, with council-owned high-rise flats. It is still an area of high social need, with the added modern problems of drugs and drug-related crime. When Hillfields Nursery Centre opened in 1971, there were plenty of jobs for local residents, and childminders and other day-care provision were scarce or non-existent.

Hillfields was the first attempt in Britain since the war to bring day-care, run by social services, and nursery education together in one combined establishment. The nursery centre was a big step forward. It offered day-care with education to children of any local residents, not just those who had been identified as having particular needs. The centre was open from seven in the morning to six at night, and many children came for breakfast and stayed until after tea.

But in the early 1980s jobs for local residents began to disappear. Sheila Thorpe, the present head of the centre, who joined the staff as deputy head in 1982, and took over as head in 1989, became increasingly aware that the service the centre offered was no longer really meeting the current needs of parents. The centre provided good quality day-care and education for children. But it did little else to support parents, build their confidence, or promote their understanding of their children's needs.

So the senior staff searched for a way to support parents as well as children. In 1987 they changed the emphasis from day-care to 'shared care'. Most families would start by coming to sessions at the centre for parents with babies and toddlers. Children over two might then be offered nursery places, where they could stay on their own for a few sessions each week. If they did not have a nursery place, they could still come to the centre with their parents.

The workers in the 'Rainbow' area, for parents and children together, set out to develop social and educational activities for the parents, as well as opportunities for young children to learn and play. They could offer informal support and advice during sessions, and had the right contacts if parents agreed they wanted more expert help. Parents could also support each other, and develop neighbourly networks to replace missing extended families. (See Box 2.1)

Box 2.1   Aims of the Hillfields Nursery Centre

The general aim of the centre is to meet the needs of the Hillfields community, and in particular the needs of under-fives and their families.
We aim:

- To provide a secure and stimulating environment in friendly surroundings, fostering quality play and language for children within a flexible programme of 'shared care' with the parents.
- To give support to parents within the centre, so that they may enjoy being with their children and enter into partnership with us. Through discussion, mutual support, advice and help, an interesting programme is devised.
- To offer outreach support in the home.
- To provide learning opportunities for each child to reach his/her full potential through meaningful and planned play activities, both informal and formal.
- To provide opportunities for parents to make relationships among themselves

---

The centre brought together families from a very multi-ethnic community: in 1996 half the families were of white British origin, a quarter of the children in the centre were from families with a variety of Asian origins, 15 per cent had black African-Caribbean origins, and ten per cent had mixed origins. Its well-embedded multicultural emphasis is visible to any visitor, in displays on the walls, children's work, and the team of bilingual assistants chatting to parents and working with children.

At first some workers had serious doubts that parents, used to being offered full day-care places, would welcome the change to shared care. But the Rainbow system turned out to be very popular. By the mid 1990s, Rainbow was catering for up to 140 children and their parents each week, and many of the parents were attending groups and classes. Since local unemployment was about 40 per cent in 1996, there was little demand for five days a week day-care – and great need for a convivial centre for parents to meet and make friends and have non-judgmental advice on tap.

Many children who start in Rainbow move on to the main nursery, which is divided into two sections, Woodlands, for two- to three-year-olds, and Treetops, for threes to fives. Neither operates a conventional five part time sessions a week. The aim is to fit in with parents' needs as flexibly as possible, while trying to meet the high level of demand for places. The whole centre continued to stay open all year round.

These arrangements have been very successful over the past ten years. However they are not set in concrete. Hillfields, under its present management, will continue to try to respond to new needs of the community if they emerge. It has developed more structured access-type courses to start parents along the road to marketable qualifications and jobs.

In 1996, unemployment was still very high, but there were indications that life was getting a little easier for some families. Numbers of nursery children qualifying for free dinners were slightly down (there were 88 in 1996). If a demand for more full day-care returned, Hillfields has the flexibility to adapt. At present the centre is open between 8.15 and 5.00, but the majority of children attend between 9.00 and 3.45. However it is possible for parents to arrange longer sessions when they need them, and contact meetings for families with school-age children regularly take place after 3.45.

In recent years local schools have been increasing their provision for under fives, and some have started 'wraparound' extended day services. In 1996, the city launched a major pre-school initiative for three to five-year-olds. But there is still very little high quality provision for under threes, and the city's education department continues to recognise the value of the work done at Hillfields with relatively generous funding.

The building

Hillfields was purpose-built as a combined centre, with spaces for babies and children of different age groups. These days it is bursting at the seams with all the activities that it houses. The Rainbow area is a big room, with scattered chairs for adults, a sofa at one end, good for reading with a small group of children, and a lot of toys and equipment – sand and water, and art and construction materials. A laundry and changing area for babies leads off the main room. There are doors out onto one of the centre's two gardens.

Across the corridor there is a room with two cookers and comfortable chairs, which is used for cookery and other groups for adults, cooking with the nursery children, and special events – on my visit a seven year old girl, who was at the centre for a contact visit with her parents, was having a birthday party. A separate room has been fitted out as a soft play and activity area, and is used by children in the Rainbow parent and toddler groups and the nursery children. It is also used when there is a creche for parents attending groups, and for mother and baby sessions.

Woodlands, the nursery for two to three-year-olds, has its own garden. It has a reasonably large room (the centre is short of space all round) with two smaller rooms leading off it. Treetops, the nursery for the older children, has a long narrow space, and shares the larger of the two gardens with the children in Rainbow. There is a general office, and four smaller offices for the administrator and the three senior staff, which are sometimes also used for the meetings of the three staff teams. The staffroom doubles as a bigger meeting room, and is used for the many social services case conferences that take place on the premises.

Rainbow

Rainbow opened with two family workers. By 1996, it had grown so much there were six, plus bilingual assistants who between them speak all four main Asian community languages. Most of the workers also ran groups for adults. There are sessions for parents with babies and toddlers five mornings and three afternoons a week. Parents can stay for lunch for £1 a head every day (lunches are free for children qualifying for free school meals). When parents first come in, the workers try to find a session or sessions that fit their schedules – but no one is turned away if they need support at any time.

One of the workers concentrates on the children, working alongside them. The other workers spend most of their time chatting to parents. It is all very informal – general discussions develop naturally about children, or about current interests. I was there during Ramadan, and heard a Muslim mother explaining how it was observed, and what the rules were, to a small interested group of workers and parents. The bilingual assistants are available for both children and adults: their presence since they were first appointed in 1991 has greatly increased the use of the Rainbow facilities by members of the local Asian communities.

Each session has a snack time, and a group time when children have a song, story or discussion. Children who stay to lunch sit sociably round a table, and parents said they were surprised and pleased how quickly even children who were impossible at mealtimes at home adjusted to the expected standards of behaviour. Families who might well be stigmatised by normal social services family provision can blend unobtrusively in to the well-staffed mainstream group. The informal, open-access setting is excellent for social services contact visits and assessments, and many take place there.

The Rainbow workers also run a toy library, which is open on two days a week for everyone using the centre. It has toys, puppets, books and tapes and videos, and a good collection of books and tapes in the main community languages. Toys and books cost 20p to borrow, and videos 30p.

Adult groups

The Rainbow staff also organise groups for adults. There is a special mother and baby group, where parents can discuss the particular needs of very young children. Staff bring in outsiders to meet a particular interest of the group – health visitors have run a session on weaning, and someone from the Body Shop has come in to show techniques and suitable oils for baby massage. If at any time a small group of parents seems to share difficulties over a particular aspect of their children's development or behaviour, the staff may suggest a one-off discussion group, perhaps inviting health visitors or others with special expertise to contribute.

Cookery groups are often a good starting point for getting parents involved in activities for adults. So is a very popular Friday group, which meets and plans its own affordable outings and activities – roller skating, a visit to a fire station, a Christmas lunch. As one parent said, it is good for confidence and for 'discovering there is life after children'. The groups themselves decide how they want to use the time – what to cook, where to go, what to discuss.

There are also two more structured classes that are accredited by the Central Access Network and can lead on to further education. The I CAN class – Initial caring and nurturing – was developed by Dot Watson, a member of the Hillfields staff, when she worked in a nursery in a local secondary school, together with a member of Coventry English for speakers of other languages team. The programme included work on child care and child development, health and safety and healthy eating, and adults' personal development and confidence. It also highlighted key English words and language needed for the course.

The course has now been adapted to suit any parents using the centre. There is a range of structured activities and projects to fit any level of education. 'The aim is to use the skills and knowledge people already have, and develop their English along the way', said Dot Watson. The course is accredited by the Central Access Network, through Warwick University. So is the 'step between' course, developed by the centre's own workers. The 'step' is on to more formal education, and again the students build up portfolios of writing and other work. Mothers taking the course said that, much to their surprise, they found they had enjoyed doing homework and writing essays on topics that interested them. 'It made me realise what I want to do', said one mother. 'I'm going to get GCSEs and A levels and do a B Ed at Warwick University'. Several people have moved on from these courses to further education. Some have also contributed to the work of the centre, working in the creche and running cookery classes.

The creche makes it possible for parents to attend groups, knowing that their children will be well looked after, usually by people they know. The arrangements are flexible, and if children prefer to stay in the Rainbow area or in the part of the nursery they attend on other days, the workers usually arrange it. The centre staff are careful to encourage parents to make use of other local opportunities and courses, and not try to meet all adult education needs themselves. For example there is an excellent English for speakers of other languages course elsewhere in Hillfields, which they encourage parents to attend.

Outreach

If parents want support at home, perhaps to discuss a sensitive problem or to work on strategies to improve their children's behaviour, Rainbow staff will go out to them. The centre's workers also go out to work in people's homes as part of social services children's plans. In 1996 the centre put in a successful bid to the Single Regeneration Budget for the costs of a half-time outreach worker. She will work on agreed programmes with at least ten families, who may be referred by other agencies or may refer themselves

Woodlands

Woodlands, the nursery for two- to three-year-olds, is a happy consequence of Hillfield's origin as an integrated centre. It is an unusual service for parents and children, giving parents a significant amount of time to themselves, and children a flying educational start. There are 30 children each session, looked after by five nursery officers and one teacher, who leads the team and is also the centre's special needs coordinator.

Members of staff visit families at home before children start, to explain the nursery's routines and curriculum and introduce the children's records of achievement. Parents are encouraged to stay for as long as it takes for their child to settle in, and to withdraw gradually. Most children attend for two days a week, with a mixture of part-time and all-day sessions: in 1997, 69 children altogether had places. All children who come in the morning can stay to lunch. As more children become three, the required staffing ratio moves from 1:4 to 1:6, and more children can be offered two full days at the nursery. 'It's about a lot of children having a bit of nursery experience: it is good that they are at home for a large proportion of the week at their age,' said Anna Smith, the teacher who coordinates the Woodlands team.

The nursery is furnished with homely things, like sofas where children can read and have a cuddle and take quick naps, and a toaster for snacks. The staff say they are not providing watered-down nursery schooling, but trying to meet the particular needs of the age group. A separate room has been given over to messy play, with sand and water and other tactile materials – 'very very important for this age group', said Anna Smith, the coordinator of the Woodlands team.

The curriculum is partly based on work on heuristic play, allowing children to explore the properties of materials for themselves.

(Goldschmeid 1994, Goldschmeid and Jackson 1994). There are a lot of natural things, such as pine cones and corks: Anna Smith says that the children's play with them is more open-ended and creative than it is with many manufactured toys. The staff aim to extend children's language and build up their concentration by allowing them to follow through their own interests, within the boundaries of being part of a group. Every session also has a small group time, where keyworkers take their own group for discussion and stories and songs. Many of the children have very limited experience of the world beyond inner Coventry, so there are many outings in the centre's minibus to local country parks and places of interest.

Treetops

The Treetops nursery for three- to five-year-olds is a slightly awkward set of spaces, with a narrow corridor section in the middle. It is divided into learning zones: the only separate room is used for mathematical activities, and other zones cover technology and modelling; sand and painting; fine motor and construction activities, and literacy and graphics. An area for imaginative play changes with children's current interests – it was a hospital on my visit.

Children stay for between two and four and a half days a week – in 1997, there were 56 children, filling 35 full-time equivalent places. Staff try to offer parents the number of sessions they need – those who are working or studying can usually be offered full-time places, provided the children can cope with it. In 1997, continuity with Woodlands was improved by key workers moving on to Treetops with their own groups of children. Before, the staff had found that children lost ground for a few weeks when they moved to the older group – the change meant that they kept up momentum.

The Treetops staff were focusing on getting children to plan their activities, and to discuss the results informally during lunch and small group times. The emphasis on planning seemed to be extending children's concentration – for example one child kept coming back to a model he was making because the planning process had made him clearer about what he wanted to achieve.

Curriculum and planning

The staff had been working hard on curriculum and planning for the past two years. Jackie White, the teacher who came as curriculum deputy in 1994 had had varied experience in a day nursery, as an early-years coordinator in a primary school, and as an NNEB course tutor. Her thinking had been influenced by the High/Scope approach, encouraging children to plan and review their own activities.

In both Woodlands and Treetops the staff had recently moved from offering children more directed activities to a free choice, with resources on open access for children all the time. (The approach was piloted in Treetops, and at first some of the Woodlands workers were concerned that the very young children would just tip everything out onto the floor. They were pleasantly surprised.)

In Treetops, the staff now complete planning sheets for every zone of the Treetops nursery, under the categories identified in the School Curriculum and Assessment Authority's *Desirable Outcomes* (SCAA/DfEE 1996). They highlight activities that fit children's current interests and needs, and identify learning outcomes that the activities should help to promote.

The workers spend a week at a time in each zone of the nursery. There is a small loose-leaf folder in each zone with observation sheets for the workers to note what a child did, what they said and to whom, and their level of involvement. These notes go to the key worker and the coordinator, and are used to build up each child's record of achievement. If there is any concern about a particular child, for example suspicion that they are under-achieving, the child is particularly targeted for observation.

In Woodlands the staff now keep similar observations and records, and in the Rainbow sessions, the parents and workers keep diaries of children's achievements. One result of the recent emphasis on planning and recording is that Rainbow parents become much more involved in charting and promoting their children's development, and the level of detail given in the regular feedback meetings with nursery parents is much higher.

Admissions

A panel of the head and pastoral deputy, the coordinator of Rainbow, and a local health visitor meets to decide which families on the waiting list should have nursery places. All must come from the Hillfields catchment area. The panel considers the family's and children's needs, and factors such as language and development, before deciding who will be given places.

Special needs

Anna Smith, the special needs coordinator, meets with each of the three staff teams once a month to check on the progress of children identified as having special needs. The centre has the resources to take some children with fairly acute needs – there were two with severe developmental delay, where staff worked with the children's home teachers, and a profoundly deaf child. One of the centre's workers had learnt sign language, and several others had learnt some basic signing so they could communicate with him more easily.

The staff say it is important that they do not label children as having special needs too quickly. Several whose development seems to be badly delayed have simply had very limited experiences, and blossom after a time at the centre. A speech therapist comes to the centre to work with individual children every six weeks, and feeds back information about suitable programmes to parents and staff.

Staffing, staff development and training

Hillfields has a large staff, with four teachers, 22 nursery officers (full time equivalent), six bilingual assistants (four full time equivalent) and an administrator, and support staff. Altogether there are 35 people on the staff, including part-timers and job-shares, so staff management, and working out children's and families' sessions to give them continuity of staffing, is a complicated business.

Although the teachers and nursery officers are on different contracts, there is little friction – partly because the teachers work the same hours as everyone else, and do not take their full holiday entitlement. The teachers' job is as much to work with other staff as with children, helping them to make the most of the opportunities to stimulate children's language and cognitive development.

A recent OFSTED report recommended that the centre should have more teachers, and Sheila Thorpe would like two more, one to work with parents and children in Rainbow, and one to work across the two nurseries. She would also ideally like to have a member of staff with full social work training, though the present pastoral deputy and family workers now have a great deal of experience of partnership with social services.

The bilingual assistants have been an important addition to the staff in the last three years. It had taken some persuasion to get them: there had been a view that nursery children do not really need bilingual support. However they have had an immense impact, particularly in the Rainbow area, where their presence has encouraged Asian parents, and particularly the most needy ones, to use the centre. They have also had a very good effect on children's confidence and progress in the nursery.

The head, curriculum deputy and pastoral deputy make up the senior team, and between them oversee the two nurseries and Rainbow, which each has its own coordinator. In the mid-1980s, the LEA agreed that the whole staff team should meet together every Wednesday afternoon. This gives them a much-needed three-hour session each week for planning, record-keeping, staff supervisions and training. The nursery staff teams also meet regularly once a week for planning and review sessions, and the Rainbow staff meet briefly twice a day to plan and review each session.

The staff has been able to bring in a number of high level advisers and consultants to work on a variety of curriculum topics and issues such as bilingualism. Warwick university academics have in the past been involved in the centre's management committee, and Sheila Thorpe says they were important in challenging thinking and taking the establishment forward. The centre also pays for staff to go on individual courses, often to the London Institute of Education. Recently workers have been on courses on nursery technology, science, and role play.

As a result of all the expertise and training within the centre, Hillfields is now developing its own Early Years Training centre, putting on courses for other professionals in Coventry and Warwickshire. So far, the venture has been very successful: courses such as one on leadership in the early years attracted between 40 and 50 people. The centre also acts as a training base for nursery nurses.

Links with other professionals

The community medical officer comes in once a month. She carries out children's development checks for families who want them, and is available for one-off consultations. However, centre workers also encourage parents to use their normal doctors and clinics for most medical matters.

There is a weekly link meeting between the pastoral deputy, a local health visitor and the community medical officer to discuss any current concerns or to report progress. Social services used to take part, but in recent years the local office has moved further away, and social workers have been under too much pressure to attend. However, there are excellent day-to-day links between the pastoral deputy, the Rainbow coordinator and individual social workers over work with particular families.

The Hillfields family workers in Rainbow have become regular partners with social workers for family support and assessment: the week I was there, the Rainbow coordinator had attended three case conferences. The centre is regularly used for contact meetings between children and parents.

Funding and management

Hillfields is managed by Coventry's education department. Its total budget from the local authority was £462,000 in 1996-97, of which £157,000 was recharged to social services. The centre also gets funds from other sources – the BBC's Children in Need funded the toy library, and the salary of the new outreach worker comes from the Single Regeneration budget. There is also a local benefactor, who raises about £4000 a year for the centre.

The centre was given delegated management of its budget in 1995. 'It's good to have that control: it's a psychological boost', said Sheila Thorpe. There is a management committee, with council and community representatives, three parents, staff representatives and co-opted members. It meets once a term, and the head and staff and parents' representatives make regular reports for discussion. The committee has no executive responsibility for the financial management of the centre.

Outcomes

There has been no recent research on the outcomes of the services at Hillfields. A study of Rainbow provision in 1989 found that its 'innovative' services promoted parents' self-confidence and self-esteem. They could share their skills and problems and get help, support and encouragement from staff and from each other. The report commented that these are necessary pre-conditions to being able to enjoy one's children, and to develop satisfying relationships with them and so to identify and meet their needs (Braun 1990).

The centre's staff have worked hard to communicate their needs, vision and purpose to local authority officers and councillors, who have provided good support at a time of overall cutbacks. The centre has now achieved remarkably seamless integration between the once separate elements of its service: care, education and family support. The Rainbow shared care team is able to support families according to their needs, with no distinctions or stigma. The growing experience and confidence of the family workers has clearly been of enormous value to over-stretched social services. They also seem to have been very successful in attracting all the ethnic, religious and language groups in their community.

An OFSTED report in 1996, working to the criteria set out in *Desirable Outcomes* found that the 'rich and varied' learning programme provided in the Rainbow area had a significant effect, developing positive attitudes towards learning and resulting in appropriate levels of attainment for the children's age. The report had high praise for the children's social and emotional development and behaviour, and their levels of concentration. They praised the staff's understanding of how children learn, and their enthusiasm for their work.

The inspectors felt the centre would benefit from employing more teachers to work with three- to five-year-olds, and that staff needed to pay more attention to literacy, mathematics and the creative development of the most able older children. Even so, they found attainment in those areas in line with national expectations – no mean feat in an area of inner city council housing, with considerable social problems, where many children go on to school as young four-year-olds.

In the wider context of building up the confidence of children and parents – which research has shown to be the most lasting benefit of nursery education (Sylva 1994) – the centre clearly does very well indeed. The parents using the centre could not praise it too highly. More than one described how isolated and lonely they had been, looking after children in a new neighbourhood, cut off from their families, before they discovered the centre. 'It's the only nursery that's for the mums as well as the children', said one.

The support continues after children leave the nursery – a mother who had been having trouble with her seven year old told me she went back to the family workers, who gave her a 'one on one' on behaviour management. 'He's much better now' she says. Children who have been rejected by other nurseries are made welcome. One mother was arranging to bring her epileptic nephew, who had been refused a local nursery place, in order to help the child and give her sister a break.

Several parents said their once-difficult children were now eating, behaving well – and smiling more. 'He used to hit out at anything that upset him, and throw himself on the ground screaming when we went shopping' said one mother. 'He's a wonderful little boy now.' The parents say they see the staff as friends – 'not like teachers, it's not like they're just doing a job' said one. Perhaps the best tribute of all came from a mother whose husband wants to move away from the area. 'I tell him I'm not budging, not till they've all got through nursery' she said. 'He says: "But it's only a nursery" and I tell him: "No, it's not just a nursery. It's our life".'

Box 2.2   Hillfields – summary

Strengths
- Very responsive to parents and local community.
- Seamless integration of education, care and family support.
- Support and group for parents of babies.
- Care and education for two to threes, as well as three to fives.
- Strong leadership.
- Excellent bilingual support for parents and children.
- Excellent links with health services and successful partnership with social services.
- Good links with other community projects.
- Early years training centre.

But
- Has not been replicated locally: seen as expensive.

Table 3.1   The Patmore Centre, London

Services for children	Services for adults and the community	Links with other professionals	Funding and management
Flexible day care between 8.30am and 6.00pm.	Basic education – literacy and numeracy.	Joint community projects.	Managed by Save the Children.
Creche	Advice and advocacy.	Good links with further education colleges.	No management committee (but appropriate steering groups for all local projects).
	NVQ assessment centre. Launched mentoring scheme for childminders and other carers wanting NVQ qualifications.	Regular visits by doctor: development checks and immunisation.	Main funder has been Save the Children (£227,000, 1995–96). Also funding from Wandsworth Social Services, and £55,000 from fee income.
	Promoter of community development projects (implemented in partnership with other agencies) – eg babysitting exchange, play scheme.	Base for social workers' work with children. Participation in social services assessments.	But in late 1996, funding in jeopardy after Save the Children cutbacks.
	Family literacy work in social services family centres and school.		

3.   The Patmore Centre, London

Introduction

Until very recently, the Patmore estate in Wandsworth provided bottom-of-the-heap housing for families who, the moment they were moved into the estate, started trying to move out again. Many families led isolated lives, fearful of their neighbours. The 1991 census showed a very young population – 32 per cent of residents were under 16, and more than half the children lived in single parent households. Seventy-three per cent of the households with children had no central heating, and many of the flats were damp. Two thirds of the households had no car. Twenty-eight per cent of the adults were unemployed – two and a half times the number in both Wandsworth and London as a whole.

In the mid 1970s, the Save the Children Fund took over a ground floor flat in the estate, and opened a children's centre. At the time – and for some 15 years to come – it was to be the only support service for Patmore residents based in the estate. The centre ran a nursery for children, a drop-in creche, and support and advice services for parents. In 1987, Save the Children undertook a major review of the work of the centre, and found it was doing an excellent job in very inadequate premises. The charity decided to raise funds for a new purpose-designed base on the estate, on land rented from Wandsworth.

The new purpose-built Patmore Centre opened in 1991 (it won a Royal Institution of British Architects award for community architecture). Staff were now able to expand their work in child care, community development, and education and training for adults. The single-story building has space for a 25-place day nursery, a creche, adult education and meeting rooms, and a base for advice work.

In the last five years, life on the Patmore estate has begun to improve. Central heating has been installed in most flats and houses (though many families still can't afford to run it). There are now housing cooperatives and other agencies with offices on site. The population is becoming less nomadic: families are beginning to stay put.

Sadly, funding problems and changing priorities at Save the Children have meant that in 1997 the work of the Patmore Centre, as described here, may have to be radically restructured, or even stop altogether. The Patmore story will remain a model of what can be achieved in a community-based project with a range of services developing around a high quality nursery, but the work itself may not be able to continue.

Community development

Perhaps the most unusual feature of the Patmore Centre is that, along-side its services for children and parents, it has a full-time, community development officer on the staff. Funke Fadayomi, who had worked in Wandsworth for many years, joined the centre just before the move to the new building. Much of her work was with individuals, offering advice, support and advocacy. Women with violent partners, people having problems with benefits and allowances, child protection and child custody cases, and many other issues turn up in her small office, with its rows of tidy, clearly labelled files of information on open shelves. 'I need a lot of information on tap, and it helps people to see that I know my stuff', she said.

On behalf of her clients, she is prepared to badger the benefits agency, or the social services offices in two boroughs (the Patmore Centre is near the border between Wandsworth and Lambeth, and there can be buck-passing when, for example, a Wandsworth resident flees from domestic violence to a refuge in Lambeth). But she also helps her clients become more self-confident and independent in tackling problems for themselves. At first, in a crisis, she does the telephoning, while they listen. Then she gets them to telephone from her office, where she can take over if they lose the plot. She teaches them to take notes of conversations, and keep careful records. 'When you give people a lot of attention at a critical period, they become more self-confident and much less demanding' she said.

One important strand of her work has been advocacy for people who do not speak fluent English, and who can be trapped by their inability to convey complications and nuances. 'They can answer "yes" and "no" but not "yes, but . . . " As well as one-to-one work, her presence on the local estates has been an important catalyst. The Patmore centre's approach to project development is to bring agencies together and build partnerships. 'We would never start a piece of work without calling a multi-agency meeting, even if we're confident there's a need for it', said Sue Emerson, the centre's project manager.

In recent years a number of projects have developed from the centre staff's grass-roots knowledge of life, and people's needs, on the local estates. One of the most recent was a baby-sitting exchange. Many parents on the estate did not have the network of friends and trusted neighbours needed for informal baby-sitting arrangements. Worried about child abuse, they thought it safer to leave children on their own rather than get in a stranger to look after them. The Patmore Centre organised a survey to find out the scale of the problem, brought together professional workers, and called a meeting to get something going. The Department of Health agreed to fund a one-year pilot project.

Parents and volunteer carers were recruited, and given 16 hours training at the centre. The training was attractive to people who did not themselves need baby-sitters, but were interested in future jobs in child care. It covered topics like child protection, children's emotional development, age-appropriate play, and health and safety, including basic first aid. Centre staff, and other appropriate professionals, ran the sessions. One year is a very short time to move from scratch to a fully fledged volunteer-run system. But even so at the end of the scheme, when the funding for the full-time coordinator was running out, volunteers were beginning to take over the administration, and the scheme was off to a good start.

Another Patmore initiative provided more activities for older children on the estate, with the centre again bringing together a variety of agencies and people, including local young people, to address the problem. In 1996 a successful Save the Children bid to the National Lottery provided funds to train local young people to research needs and possibilities. Funke Fadayomi and a local health visitor were also working to set up a local family planning centre, with a particular emphasis on providing young people with information on sexual health. 'I've had to support too many teenage mothers' she said. They have received some funding from the Community Health Trust, but so far nothing concrete had happened. 'It's not giving up, you see', she said. 'I'm not prepared to see four years' work going down the Swanee. My job is to persist.'

Education and training

One of the original aims for the new building was to provide basic skills training for women in the local area, to increase their access to further education and training, and in particular to increase access to childcare training. An education and training coordinator, Lina Fajerman, was appointed in 1991 to implement the brief. The centre staff knew that although there were three colleges within walking distance, many women on the estate did not have the confidence to go and sign on to basic education courses. Family circumstances often meant that in any case, a course requiring regular attendance wasn't feasible.

The centre therefore started a 'Stepping Out Open Learning' course in basic communication skills, where women could pursue an individual learning plan at their own pace. Because the course was at the centre, nursery parents could easily drop in and find out about it. There was a good creche on the premises for parents taking part. Participants could study for City and Guilds Wordpower and Numberpower qualifications, building individual portfolios following individual needs and interests. They could focus on their particular needs: some might want to work on writing official letters, others on basic spelling.

The important thing about the scheme is its flexibility. Staff can help women to assess their needs. They can steer the more confident straight on to local colleges, and work one-to-one to get the least confident started. When there are severe family difficulties, such as a violent relationship, the women get support. 'I cajole and bully quite a lot, phoning people if they don't come in', said Lina Fajerman. 'Things are often very turbulent in their lives'.

Once the approach had been tested, the Patmore workers approached Wandsworth Social Services and the Adult Learning Basic Skills Unit (now the Basic Skills Agency) and together they launched a project to extend the approach to parents in Wandsworth's Social Services children's centres (which provide for children and families whose difficulties are judged to need social services intervention). The response to the scheme was very good. Participants said they had found it interesting, and gained in self-confidence. The scheme had helped them to go to college, and get jobs. 'It set me free', said one woman. Another said 'If we get on with our reading and writing we can teach our kids as well'.

The staff in the children's centres said the classes had made a real difference to the participants, giving them self confidence – 'children always benefit when parents feel better about themselves' commented one centre – and making them much more willing to discuss problems and look for solutions. At the end of the pilot year, South Thames College took on the scheme, and provided a tutor to coordinate it. Open learning classes were still running at the Patmore Centre. When I was there, there were two Open Learning sessions a week at the centre, one mainly for women learning English as a second language, and the other for people wanting help with basic literacy and numeracy.

At the time of my visit in 1996, the Patmore staff were hoping to develop new family literacy and parent support projects in Wandsworth and neighbouring London boroughs, always in partnership with other agencies. Lina Fajerman (now working mainly for a division of Save the Children, but also keeping a base at Patmore) had started a project with a Wandsworth primary school: a number of parents had been very keen to take part, a college could provide a tutor, but funds were needed for a creche, and for a coordinator for ten days a year. They were also hoping to pilot a 'supporting parents supporting children' project. The idea was to recruit and train members of ethnic minority groups to support parents of 0-2-year-olds.

The Patmore Centre had also been closely involved in setting up a local NVQ assessment centre for child care and education. The staff were concerned about local self-employed childcare workers, such as childminders. In theory they could use NVQ to accredit and extend their experience. But it was almost impossible in practice, with no employer to support them, and no possibility of taking a full-time course. For such people, the NVQ system can present an insuperable set of hurdles. The centre brought together a number of relevant agencies, such as South Thames College, the Wandsworth Play Association, the Wandsworth Childminding Association, and Wandsworth Adult College.

They designed a pilot project to find and train 'mentors' who could work with groups of isolated carers, and help them achieve NVQ qualifications. The local Training and Educational Council, AZTEC, the Baring Foundation, and the Basic Skills Agency offered funding. The mentors could translate the impenetrable jargon of NVQ performance criteria for the candidates, help them to structure and complete portfolios, help them with the skills needed to write reports and case studies and child observations, and generally encourage them. Not everyone completed the course; several decided after the first exploratory stage that NVQs were not for them. The cost of NVQ assessment turned out to be the biggest deterrent. But over 40 per cent of those who signed on for the second stage of the project, aiming at an NVQ, were successful. Having proved itself, the mentor system has now been adopted by local colleges, and Save the Children has published a practical guide to running a mentor scheme.

All these projects are good examples of the Patmore approach to project development: partnership with other agencies; involvement of local professionals in different services; the establishment of a multi-agency steering group; and careful published evaluation.

The children's centre

The children's centre is an all-day nursery for 25 children, open for 50 weeks of the year. Apart from two or three places reserved by social services for families with particular priority needs, anyone living in the catchment area can apply for a place. Admissions are by waiting list: the list is closed when there are 60 names, but the demand is even higher. Children with special needs are welcome if parents choose the centre rather than one of Wandsworth's specialist facilities. The centre has accommodated children with hearing, speech and visual disabilities, and autism.

The centre does not have to advertise: its reputation spreads by word of mouth. The ethnic mix of children has varied as the nomadic populations on the estate changed. There have been large groups of Filipinos and Vietnamese in the past. In 1996 the majority of families using the centre came from a variety of black African backgrounds. The nursery has to charge parents for its services. Until 1996 the charge was 50p an hour, or about £27.50 a week, plus a notional charge for meals. That can be a big chunk of the parent's earnings, which average about £110 a week, but it's a great deal cheaper than local childminders, who charge about £65 a week. The real cost of a Patmore nursery place was £146 a week in 1996.

The children's services coordinator, Kim Buckingham, was an experienced social services day nursery manager before she arrived at the centre soon after the new building opened. There are six early years development workers, who work two shifts, 8.15 to 4.15 and 10.00 to 6.00. The excellent staffing ratio is necessary because the centre takes two- to three-year-olds. In recent years, many families have chosen to move children on to nursery classes at three or to reception classes soon after they are four. The school places are free, but parents also feared they would miss out on places at the more popular primary schools unless they got their children in early. Staff were concerned that the advent of vouchers in Wandsworth would intensify the competition from schools for young four-year-olds. But in practice, in September 1996 several parents decided to leave their children at Patmore. The hours offered by the centre are ideal for working parents, and the staffing ratio and careful curriculum planning are attractive to parents.

There is no fully qualified early years teacher on the staff, though one of the nursery workers had Montessori training. The centre's workers have a variety of qualifications, such as NNEB, diplomas in child care and Pre-school Playgroup Association courses. Some of them started as volunteers, moved on to become 'sessional staff', paid to cover the permanent staff, and have gained qualifications on the job. All the nursery workers have contributed to an interesting home-grown curriculum and record keeping system, geared to encouraging and monitoring the development of two- and three-year-olds as well as any four-year-olds who stay on.

The day begins at about 8.30 for children, with breakfast – costing 20p – for children who want it. The attractive dining room is also used as an area for learning: in summer 1996 the curriculum theme was 'The Body', and the dining room had displays of healthy and unhealthy food, brought in by the children, and a huge diagram of the digestive system with all the parts labelled – mouth, tongue, oesophagus, stomach, small intestine, large intestine. The nursery workers pay a lot of attention to extending children's vocabulary, and the children love long words like oesophagus. Breakfast is a relaxed occasion, when parents dropping their children can sit down and chat with Kim Buckingham or other staff over a cup of coffee. Relations with the parents are visibly warm, with terrific jokes and parents weeping on the nursery workers' shoulders. It probably helps a lot that the ethnic mix of the staff reflects the ethnic mix of the families.

Breakfast goes on until 9.20, and children then move into the main nursery, which has a big central space, an art room, a 'quiet room' for stories and music and naps, and a 'consultancy room' for small group work, for example a 'rising fives' group of children who are ready for more formal work on writing or number. There is also a hard-surfaced play area, with some climbing equipment (on my visit the centre's mini-bus was the most popular piece of play equipment: children were going on elaborate fantasy journeys to Florida and the West Indies).

There are two story sessions a day, with different stories for younger and older children. At ten o'clock, the staff organise activities round the curriculum theme of the moment: for The Body, when I was there, there were hairdressing, collage faces on paper plates, and a health and hygiene focus in the bathroom. The kitchen was used for healthy cooking. Children have lunch with their keyworkers, unless they choose to sit with a friend from another group. The afternoon has its own routine, with naps, the second story, singing sessions, and plenty of free play that the staff join in unobtrusively, extending children's ideas and vocabulary. Since parents pick up children at different times, there is again plenty of opportunity for chat with staff and informal discussions about children.

Curriculum and parent involvement

The nursery team had done a lot of recent work on curriculum, and it shows. Parents are an important part of the process. Most early years practitioners pay lip service to parents being the 'prime educators' of their children. At Patmore they have made sure the rhetoric is real. The Patmore curriculum is planned and monitored under five headings: physical, intellectual, language, emotional and social development. Parents are given a booklet when their children start, explaining the approach, emphasising that children learn all the time: 'no single setting is more appropriate for learning than another'.

The nursery workers choose a curriculum theme, and plan in some detail how it will be pursued by different members of staff in the different parts of the nursery. In the planning, they keep an eye on OFSTED's *Desirable Outcomes* and the requirements of Key Stage One of the national curriculum. Often, the theme comes out of children's or parents' questions and suggestions. Before they complete plans for a theme, the staff give parents clear written information and a questionnaire, so they can make suggestions or query any aspect. For 'The Body', questions included whether parents would mind if medical terms for parts of the body were used; if they would mind children seeing diagrams, for example of the foetus; if they minded answering questions their children might come home with.

Box 3.1   Extracts from the Patmore Centre's Good Practice Guidelines

Children are individuals and need respect. They have the right to hold their own views, and should be encouraged to do so. An adult only has the right to stop children experimenting if it is harmful to themselves or others.

Punishment which hurts, frightens or humiliates children is unacceptable, as well as being ineffective. Smacking, shoving and 'naughty' chairs or corners only asserts the adult's power over children, without helping them to improve. We should give children time out when they behave badly, or have disrupted an activity. . .

Children who misbehave in order to seek adult attention are clearly not getting enough attention. On occasions when they have been good, or helped their peers, staff should praise and encourage the child, so that the child realises that good behaviour also gains attention and, at times, rewards.

If a child is upset or angry with you, there is no shame in asking for another adult to intervene. It is important, if this has happened, to return to the child after you have taken time out, to rebuild the relationship.

Adults should not force-feed children. Children are not obliged to eat the food. The carer should notify the parent if the child has not eaten during the day.

The information made it clear that staff would not go into details of human reproduction: 'This is where you will be involved in answering questions', and that the theme was chosen because of young children's great interest in their own bodies. It explained how the work would help prepare children for school, covering some human biology, and promoting language and mathematical development (the latter partly through cooking, cutting up fruit into halves and quarters and measuring liquids), hand-eye coordination, and social and emotional education, for example helping children to understand cultural differences in diet. It is an impressive amount of explanation and involvement for parents in curriculum, on top of all the day-to-day chances for informal discussion. Parents are also asked for any help they can give with the theme – sending in objects, and providing stories and background knowledge.

The staff make it clear to all parents and any volunteers and sessional staff who work with the children that a crucial part of the curriculum is the way adults treat both each other and children. Staff have drawn up brief 'Good Practice Guidelines' for everyone involved in the centre. One and a half pages of very large print outline how children must be treated and respected. (See Box 3.1.) The Patmore early years workers are visibly proud of their home-grown curriculum development. In 1996, they were beginning to explore ways of giving children even more opportunities to make and negotiate their own choices – for example moving from a set snack time to allowing children to choose when to have a drink and snack.

Planning and record keeping

The curriculum is backed by an elaborate system of observation and record keeping by keyworkers for their group of four or five children. They discuss the records with parents after three months, nine months and 15 months. They then arrange an 'exit interview' where the keyworker draws up a final record which, if parents agree, goes on to the child's primary school. The record for the first three months is about how children settle into the nursery – relations with the keyworker, other staff and children, general adjustment to the nursery, any fears and dislikes.

After that the staff use detailed checklists of performance criteria, completing a full set before every meeting with parents. Boxes are coloured yellow, blue or red, depending on whether a child hasn't begun on a particular criterion, is trying, or is competent. The idea is to have a quick visual guide to the progress children have made. There are a number of categories, with about 25 items on each. So for spoken language, staff record whether the child can use 'yesterday and tomorrow', whether they use words for movement – such as 'through', 'away', 'from' – accurately, and whether they use regular past tenses and correct pronouns.

'It seems a lot to cover but it's quite easy. You observe the children doing things – James was riding a bike – and note it on the checklist in the evening' said a nursery worker. For some items – such as ability to finish a puzzle, or to count to ten or 20 – the staff keep special equipment ready for children to try. They say children rather like 'doing their checklist.' Parents get involved, too. Some use the checklists to record children's new achievements at home, others keep notes, while others just tell staff about things children can now do.

The creche

The centre used to have a creche, and the curriculum planning and record keeping extended to the babies and younger children using it. But budget cuts (see *Funding management and the future of the centre*, below) meant the creche had to be closed, losing good and committed staff and a valuable service to parents. The centre could only maintain a skeleton service for people coming to adult classes. However, not entirely daunted, by summer 1996 the staff had managed to arrange for a mother and toddler group, and a creche to give parents some time off, using volunteer workers from the community. With the centre's record of training and developing child care skills, the volunteers can also offer a high-quality service.

Relations with other professionals

Other professionals use the centre as a base. A doctor comes at regular intervals to do pre-school immunisation boosters, and development checks when parents want them. Social workers use the centre to meet families, observe children, and liaise with keyworkers. The staff write reports for case conferences, and take part in assessments. There is also plenty of informal consultation: the centre is known for its long experience working with the local community.

However, more than one of the senior staff expressed some resentment at the way some professionals in the statutory sector treat even very experienced workers in the voluntary sector. They say, for example, that some social workers and others are quick to ask for help in getting alongside families when they need it – but slow to accept the professionalism and judgement of the centre workers when a request goes the other way.

Staff training and development

The centre acts as a training base both for its own staff, and for others. The staff has benefited both from a strong Save the Children Fund interest in training, and from its own project team's awareness of the importance of staff development. Some of the nursery workers started as volunteers, and have gradually moved on to being sessional workers and then joining the staff full-time. The centre has met their training needs with various courses. The workers have a demanding brief: 'They are expected to understand child development, put things on paper for parents, monitor new developments, communicate verbally and in writing, and write reports for case conferences' said Sue Emerson.

So the centre is prepared to provide a wide range of training, from help with writing reports to advanced diploma courses. At least one member of staff does a long-term course every year, with some time off for studying. Staff have done advanced diplomas in child care and education, NNEB courses, and urban studies diplomas while working at the centre. There has also been a lot of internal training for staff, with sessions on the Children Act, child protection, team-building, and many more. The centre closes for training six days a year.

Every worker has a line manager, and regular supervision sessions. All the nursery staff have two sessions with the children's services manager every month, one to discuss their personal performance and needs, and one to discuss the progress of the children in their keyworker group. The project manager's line manager is an assistant divisional director at Save the Children. The nursery staff also have a formal meeting, with agendas and minutes, once a week, when sessional staff come in to look after the children. The project coordinators meet every two to three weeks, and there is an evening meeting for all staff every six to eight weeks. There is a careful induction programme for new staff, and also for sessional staff and volunteers who work in the children's centre, trying to make sure that the ethos of the place is well understood.

The centre offers practice places for students on BTEC, NVQ, Pre-School Learning Alliance (formerly PPA) and other courses in local colleges. The children's services coordinator, Kim Buckingham, who is in charge of the nursery and creche, herself tutors at Lambeth and South Thames colleges, and is an NVQ assessor, while the project coordinator is an NVQ internal verifier. Students gaining experience at the centre are well looked after: the deputy director, who is also one of the nursery workers, is responsible for training arrangements and another nursery worker looks after students on a day-to-day basis.

Relations with Save the Children

The relationship with Save the Children has clearly been close, productive and two-way. Patmore staff have been members of various groups within the charity – groups on health issues, training issues, and cross-project meetings where experience can be shared. One of the early years development workers was a member of the good practice group. Save the Children's Equality Learning centre has offered resources, training and support, and senior staff said the project's SCF line manager has been accessible, knowledgeable and supportive. The ethos of Save the Children, valuing children's rights and participation, has been fundamental to the centre's work.

On the other side, the Patmore's convenient inner London location has been very useful to Save the Children and its fund-raisers, offering an excellent working model of the charity's aims and successful operations. Senior staff saw it as part of their job to publicise and explain the work of the charity as well as that of the centre.

Funding, management, and the future of the centre

The centre is managed by Save the Children. There is no management committee, although every individual project launched within the centre has an appropriate steering group. Save the Children has provided the great bulk of the funding so far. However, life has been particularly tough in the voluntary sector in recent years. Due to its own financial difficulties, Save the Children successively cut back the Patmore Centre's grant, with cuts of £10,000 in 1994-95, and £30,000 in 1995-96. The creche had to go, and the Education and Training coordinator took a more general role within SCF, as well as continuing part-time at Patmore.

In 1995-96 the SCF grant was £227,700. Wandsworth Social Services Department gave a grant of £55,000 (£17K of which went straight back to the council as rent), and a grant of £13,000 to pay for three nursery places for children from their 'priority list'. Fees brought in £55,000. By mid 1996, continuing financial difficulties at Save the Children meant that in 1996 the project coordinator had to find a way to re-structure the centre so that it could survive a further cut of £50K to £100K in the next financial year.

Sue Emerson put a proposal to Wandsworth – with some encouragement from Wandsworth council officers. She asked social services to increase the number of children from their 'priority list', bringing in a further £25,000. She applied to the education department for funding for a post of education, literacy and learning coordinator, working with schools and others to build on the centre's growing expertise in adult education and family literacy schemes. The proposal seemed to fit other Wandsworth priorities in education and literacy. This would have reduced the SCF contribution to £154,000. Any further cuts could have been met by shortening the nursery day.

But at the time Save the Children were changing their priorities. In future they wanted to fund development teams to work for a limited period in an area, rather than meeting the recurrent costs of permanent community projects such as Patmore. In the light of the uncertainties caused by this policy change, Wandsworth decided that they could not immediately support the restructuring plan, and decided to reduce even the borough's existing contribution to the centre.

At the time of writing (autumn 1996), the centre's funding from SCF and Wandsworth was assured only until the summer of 1997. The project team hoped that funds would still be available to continue some of the work until the summer of 1998. Discussions with Wandsworth were continuing. But unless a new source of funding could be found, the nursery would have to close in the summer of 1997. Parents had to be warned of the situation – just when many had decided to leave their four-year-olds in the nursery since it successfully met their own and their children's needs. It might be possible to develop other services in the building. But it was designed with the open-access, high quality nursery as the central hub of the project, drawing in the community and allowing other services to develop which met real needs, and could be offered with no stigma attached.

Sue Emerson – who has now also moved on to a wider role within SCF, as well as managing the Patmore Centre – and the project team were continuing to search for solutions to this impasse. But inevitably, all the uncertainty was taking its toll on the morale of a thriving centre, whose work in community development, adult education, advocacy, family literacy and child care and education had not only served and strengthened children and adults in its very disadvantaged local community, but had also informed and influenced many projects and people both within Wandsworth and neighbouring boroughs, and much further afield.

Box 3.2   The Patmore Centre – summary

Strengths
- Responsive to community needs
- Community development, in partnership with other agencies
- Quality day care with good parent involvement
- Adult education and training
- Pro-active work in child care training and family literacy
- Multiethnic staff, reflecting community

But
- No secure funding
- No formal education involvement

Table 4.1   Netherton Park Family Centre

Services for children	Services for parents and adults	Links with other professionals	Funding and management
Nursery school with some full-time places.	Drop-in and parent and toddler sessions.	Social worker linked to centre, and visits regularly.	Funded by a partnership of NCH Action for Children and the local authority. NCH pays £20,000 a year, the Education Department £97,000 a year and Social Services £41,000.
After school care for nursery and primary children.	A variety of groups and classes at the centre and at the nearby community college, including access course for further education, and classes for Asian women.	Health visitors run occasional groups.	
Parent and toddler and pre-nursery group.		Good links with local community college.	20-year service level agreement between the partners.
Holiday scheme for three to 11-year-olds.	Family support team.	Dental Hygienist visits.	
Semi-integrated nurture group for children with special needs.		Has established regular meetings for local professionals.	Management committee with three partners represented. Most line management by NCH.
			Non-executive project committee with wider parent and community membership.

4.   Netherton Park Family Centre, Dudley

Introduction

The Netherton Park Family Centre is a fine example of what can be achieved in the 1990s when someone has a clear vision, and different agencies are willing to get together to make it a reality. One or two members of staff who saw the recent transformation of a small nursery school into a thriving purpose-built family centre even call it a miracle.

Netherton is in the heart of the Black Country, near the centre of the town of Dudley. It's an area where long-established local working class families live in small industrial cottages and old housing estates, and newer medium rise estates and housing association developments have brought in a variety of newcomers, many with acute social needs. On all the indices for social and economic deprivation – unemployment, single parents, child protection – central Dudley and Netherton score well above the average for the local authority as a whole.

In 1981 Chris Catanach took over as head of a traditional nursery school housed in a building seen as temporary when it opened before World War II. She had successfully taught the whole primary school range, mainly in the East End of London. But she had become increasingly interested in the foundations for learning – the cognitive and language base necessary for children to make real academic progress.

'I wanted to do early years education properly,' she says. Doing it properly meant involving parents, particularly in an area where many families live under considerable economic and social strain. 'However "good" our practice is, it will all wash out at the end of the day if we don't get the parents in'. It also meant linking with other services dealing with young children. At the time, communication between the nursery school, social workers and health visitors was minimal – even when all the services were dealing with the same children and families.

Two years later, in 1983, the local authority threatened to close the school. Parents were up in arms, there was a great campaign, and the school was saved by the vote of just one councillor. That same year, Chris Catanach wrote her first paper to the chief education officer, calling for a community room to allow the nursery to expand its services to parents. She also set about building links with like-minded professionals in health, social services and voluntary agencies, to make sure that the needs of young children were well served.

They started what became the under eights focus, a group which at full strength involved up to 18 Dudley professionals from various services working with children. The Focus showed their muscle and range at their first 'zoo day', now an annual event, when 5000 children and adults from schools, playgroups, nurseries and voluntary projects descended on Dudley zoo for a well-planned educational day out.

At that point the Children Act 'fell like a plum into my lap', says Chris Catanach. She and the social services development officer for under-eights got the job of coordinating Dudley's Section 19 review, looking at services for young children across the board, and planning for action. They researched the socio-economic data, proving the high level of need in central Dudley and Netherton. They then conducted their own survey of parents in reception classes in those areas to find out what services the parents of young children actually wanted.

What they wanted became the basis of the Netherton Park Family Centre: a place offering nursery education – 'not just somewhere to dump children', as one mother put it – drop-in facilities for younger children; and general support and services for parents. The local authority had already decided to build a free-standing community room for the nursery school (it opened in 1990). It now agreed to spend a further £250,000 for a new building for the whole family centre project – only to postpone the project four years running when money ran out.

It became apparent that some matching external funding had to be found. Someone suggested contacting the NCH Action for Children charity. Its managers had a lot of experience running centres dealing with families in difficulties. They were interested in setting up a more open centre with a strong mainstream education element, which would make the support offered much more acceptable to parents in trouble.

The end was in sight. There were still plenty of alarms when ground-rules suddenly changed, and bigger contributions had to be levered out of tight local authority budgets. But key officers in both the charity and the local authority were solid in support. Dudley raised its contribution to £336,000, and in September 1995 the family centre opened in a purpose-designed building next to the old nursery school site. Its aims are outlined in Box 4.1.

The management partnership

NCH Action for Children manages the new family centre, and pays £20,500 a year (at 1995–96 rates) towards its running costs. Dudley's education department provides £63,950 to cover salaries for the nursery

---

Box 4.1   Aims of Netherton Park

Aims

To develop a collaborative model of quality day care provision which is accessible to all local families. To cater for the varying needs both of children and their carers in an integrated setting, without incurring social stigma. Where a specialist family need is identified, support is given in the form of flexible packages of care to help and enable parents to care for their children adequately through particularly difficult periods.

Objectives

- To acknowledge and encourage partnership and involvement with all families with young children in the area.
- To enhance the coping skills of families who have been assessed as in need of help, support or guidance, to enable these families to help themselves and improve family functioning so they can provide a safe, loving and stimulating environment for their children.
- To meet the broad pre-school educational needs of children attending the centre...
- To ensure children who have special needs receive an assessment and developmental experiences designed to maximise their potential, and are integrated into the rest of the centre wherever possible . . .
- To support families who are undergoing a crisis, either by the provision of day care for a short period. or by advice and information . . .
- To support children in need of protection from abuse . . .
- To raise child care standards generally by providing consultancy support, advice and training for a variety of child care workers and carers . . .
- To minimise the impact of social stigma for parents receiving support in the upbringing of their children.

---

school, and a further grant of £33,100. The social services department's grant is £41,200. The centre itself has to find a budget shortfall of £8,200 a year for 20 years, raising the money from fees and charges for services.

The objectives of the centre and the financial arrangements are set out in a Service Level Agreement between the three partners, which will run for 20 years. The partners are represented on a management committee that meets once a year for review and forward planning. There is also a project committee with much wider membership, including three users and other community representatives, which is more like the old governing body. It has no executive role but monitors the work and policies of the centre. Under NCH rules, one member of this committee has to visit unannounced once a month, and make a written report.

All management procedures – staff supervision and appraisal, the annual review – come from NCH, but the centre is still registered as a school and therefore has to meet education department and OFSTED requirements. Adding in the paperwork and procedures that come with Social Services referrals, there is a heavy bureaucratic load for a small staff.

But the partnership also brings great depth of support to the centre. Staff can tap in to training offered by all three partners, and advice and help from all three sets of officers. Maggi Scrivener, the NCH Assistant Director who is line manager for the project and was involved from the start, is pleased how well the project has gone. 'Families need a whole range of services that are easily accessed, without being passed from pillar to post.' She believes the best way to get more such services is through partnerships between agencies.

Building for integration

The building is delightful and welcoming. It's an octagonal structure with the older community room attached on one side, on the edge of a park. The main entrance leads into a small reception area, then straight into the main open-plan nursery that takes up most of the new building. Three small rooms open off the nursery. Two of them, the 'baby room' and the 'toddler room' interconnect. Those two are mainly used by the workers who support families in difficulties. The third is the base for a 'nurture group' of six pre-school children with special needs.

At the far end of the main nursery there is an administrative section with a staffroom, office and kitchen, and a room for adult groups. This leads through to the large community room, laid out so that parents are encouraged to play with their children as well as talk to each other.

The most striking thing about the main building, and about the way it is used in practice, is the easy flow from the spaces used for special needs and family support into the main nursery. The nurture group staff take their children out into the nursery – and when the door is open, nursery children can go in to play with them. The families working with the family support team often go out into the nursery to play with their children or just watch. There are also times when the toddlers in the community room come through into the main nursery, or mix in with the nursery children playing outdoors. This easy flow around and into what is still a mainstream nursery school makes Netherton Park a very comfortable place for families in difficulties – a place where integration is built into the fabric.

The community room

The community room opened in 1990, and ran several projects with variable success until the opening of the family centre in September 1995 brought new permanent staffing. When I was there, 72 parents and carers were using it every week. It is staffed by one worker, paid under Section 11 of the local government act. The job is shared between a nursery nurse, working four fifths time, and an Asian outreach worker.

On Monday, there is an open session, when anyone in the community can drop in – and large numbers often do. On Tuesdays and Wednesdays there are 'pre-nursery' groups, when 15 or so parents come in with children who are about to start in the nursery. Thursday is a parent and toddler session for parents and carers with younger children, who book in advance for the sessions. On Friday mornings and afternoons, parents can leave their 'pre-nursery' children for a taste of the real thing. The groups go out into the nursery with the community room worker, while PE equipment is set out in the community room for the nursery.

Some planned services, such as a regular toy and book library, had not fully developed in the first year. But in a very short time, the community room has become a vital starting point for users of the centre. It is the place where children, staff and parents (parents in this case might easily mean grandparents, or childminders) get to know each other, and begin informally to discuss children's education and development. In the centre's second year, this will develop into a slightly more formal arrangement for 'baseline assessment' of pre-nursery children, and discussion of curriculum targets.

Other professionals have also begun to come in and offer informal services for parents. A student health visitor started Monday sessions, discussing topics the parents had asked for, such as breast cancer and family planning. When she left, health managers, not wanting to lose a productive scheme, allocated another to take over. A dental hygienist has also made visits. The informal sessions make it easy for parents to discuss worries with the worker, or with other passing members of staff. One result is that in the centre's first year, one or two parents were beginning to refer themselves to the more intensive family support services on offer.

Family support

The family support work at the centre is handled by the deputy project manager, who was formerly deputy manager of a social services nursery, and three nursery nurses (two full time equivalent). They work with families referred by social workers and health visitors, as well as those who refer themselves. A social work manager joins the centre's head and deputy to form an allocation panel to decide whether families are suitable for places on the programme. Usually the programme is part of a shared care plan with other agencies, with clearly set objectives and expectations, and agreement on what will happen if parents do not stick to the arrangement.

In theory neither the Dudley social work department nor NCH Action for Children expected the Netherton Park team to get involved at the heavy end of child protection cases. But it is a difficult line to maintain, and the staff have been involved in some difficult cases. At least one couple who had rejected other more crisis-oriented services have found the Netherton Park ethos and approach acceptable. By all accounts the father had been very hostile and negative to begin with. The day I was there, a few weeks into the programme, he had brought in some faggots he had cooked specially for his family worker, and was happily making finger puppets for his children and taking photographs of them playing out in the nursery. He told me he liked coming because his children could play with the nursery children – a good example of the benefits of integrating special services with mainstream provision.

The staff can work with about ten families at any time. Once a family has been referred, the parents (or parent) meet with the family centre worker to agree a six week programme. The programme will often focus on child development, or behaviour management, and activities for each session are agreed. After six weeks, staff and parents review progress and if necessary set new targets. As well as working with the parents, the family workers offer 'respite' sessions when children come on their own.

The customers seem to like the service. I met a mother who had been seriously depressed. 'I was pulling my hair out: I couldn't look at nobody, speak to nobody, go nowhere' she told me. She had started by slipping in to the family support room round the side, unable to face the main building, but she was soon bringing biscuits in to the community room. She now has a part-time job and has signed on for an access course at college. 'Without coming here I wouldn't have had half the confidence to do what I've done' she says. 'They have very listening ears.'

The staff also make home visits, sometimes alongside social workers, and get involved in joint assessments. In September 1996 the social services department established regular support from a member of the local child and family team. He visits regularly, and can be brought in to help with cases where the family workers need support. There is no easy dividing line between 'heavy' child protection and 'light' family support, and the presence of an experienced social worker will strengthen the preventive work the centre can offer. Considering how new the work was to a young staff, it was astonishing how well, within a few months, they were getting alongside some difficult parents, and how cheerfully the parents seemed to accept their help.

A social work student who had been on a full-time placement in the centre for four months said: 'Its great strength is you can come in any doorway for any reason and find some service, with no stigma attached. There's no neon sign over people's heads saying: 'We're terrible parents.'

The nursery school

The nursery school has 45 places. When I was there 12 children were staying full-time, mainly because of a particular developmental or family need. In this way the centre can offer 'an element of day care' – particularly as it stays open until six for after school care of nursery and primary school children. There are three (full time equivalent) nursery nurses. On my visit, the only teacher on the staff was the project manager, and she had to lead all curriculum planning and evaluation. Later in 1996, the Education Department provided 0.4 of a teacher on secondment, who could share some of the load.

When I was there the staff were just beginning to review their curriculum planning and assessment in the light of *Desirable Outcomes* (DfEE/SCAA 1966). Many children in the nursery are a long way from those outcomes, and the staff were identifying 'stepping stones' in different curriculum areas that would help them assess children's progress towards the OFSTED targets. The nursery already had a careful system of observation and profiles, built up from pieces of children's work and photographs, as well as written comments. Soon after my visit, after two days' in-service on organisation and planning, nursery sessions on Wednesday were slightly shortened to allow for a weekly team meeting where staff could review and plan work, and discuss the progress of individual children.

The nursery is laid out in areas – creative, home play, science and technology, etc, with a big, clearly demarcated 'quiet area' in the middle. Members of staff move around the main areas of the nursery every couple of days. In their planning, they make sure they target every child in their group one day a week, planning activities in the part of the nursery they will be working to meet their particular needs. They group the children with roughly the same needs, such as language development, or social development, or extra extension, to make the task easier.

It was not easy for all the nursery staff to adapt to the new comings and goings and wider responsibilities brought by the family centre. Some have welcomed the new opportunities and challenges of a bigger team: others are less sure. But they all seemed to have coped well, and even the most doubtful said the children had been much less affected than she had: 'the more the merrier, as far as they're concerned'.

Special needs

Children with special needs integrate easily into this very open nursery. Half the children in the nursery have some kind of special educational need or noticeable developmental delay, and two were physically disabled, though mobile on their feet.

The provision for a nurture group of six children with Level 3 special educational needs (as defined by the SEN Code of Practice), is an unusual feature of Netherton Park. The children, aged two and a half to four and a half, come for four afternoons a week, and work with their own teacher and nursery nurse. The staff are part of the local authority's special needs service, which provides taxis for children whose parents cannot bring them.

They have their own room, but at times the mainstream nursery children can come in and play there, and at other times the staff go out with nurture group children to play in the main nursery, or outdoors. It makes an easy stepping stone to full integration for some children, and an excellent setting for the specialist staff to see how well they can cope in a big group.

Staff development and training

NCH Action for Children, the centre's manager, has a national system of staff supervision and appraisal, which the centre has adopted. All members of staff, including the project manager, have two-hour supervision sessions every two weeks, and an annual appraisal. NCH has agreed to pay the nursery staff extra for the supervision time, since they have so little non-contact time. NCH also offers high-quality training in areas such as child protection, play therapy, and counselling, which is available to staff alongside what the local authority education and social services departments can offer.

However, the centre is very tightly staffed indeed, and release for training outside the five in-service days is difficult. The administrator is paid to work only 25 hours in term time and 10 hours in the holidays (in fact she works much more). The centre is also used as a training base by a variety of agencies: for nursery nurse and child care courses, health visitor and social work courses. 'Working here has helped me to understand my role as a facilitator, working through other services', said a social work student.

Holiday play schemes and out-of-school care

The provision of out-of-school care for three- to 11-year-olds, both in term time and in the holidays, is seen as an important part of the centre's brief. The out-of-school care is registered for up to 24 children, and the centre and its community room make an attractive base for children to relax or do homework. The holiday schemes are very popular, booking up immediately, and Social Services reserve some places for children who need them. Parents are charged £7.50 for four half-day sessions a week, and social services £10. On Fridays, the staff who run the play schemes keep the family support ticking over through the holidays.

The scheme is staffed by the family support team, sessional work-ers, and a lot of volunteers, including parents and students. The first play scheme, in the summer of 1995, was exhausting for the staff and a huge success for children. Chris Catanach was determined to offer a scheme of real educational quality, with creative activities, outings, camps, the works. A number of parents said afterwards that their children's school work had markedly improved after they had gone to the play scheme.

In its second year, developing links between the centre and the nearby community college meant that older children on the play scheme could use the college's excellent sports and leisure facilities.

Involvement of families from ethnic minorities

At the time of my visit in 1996 the local Asian community was not using the family centre. But outreach work to offer them services and bring them in to the centre was a priority. The staff have used all possible local networks to contact local families from ethnic minorities, particularly Asians. The first result of the outreach was a popular sewing and dress-making class for Asian women, held at the local secondary school's com-munity wing, which has a creche run by the family centre's Asian outreach worker. In September 1996, an English class for speakers of other languages also opened in the centre itself.

Adult education

The partnership with the community college is likely to develop much further, to mutual benefit. The centre has surveyed its users to find out what classes they want, and some, such as computing and first aid, can best be offered at the college. Sarah Morgan, the community head there, said the link with the family centre had enabled them to tap in to a client group that they had otherwise found very hard to reach.

In the first year of the new building only one course, in family literacy, ran at the centre itself. An accredited access course for further educa-tion was also run for a group of 15 parents, based in a local school. Three of them succeeded at Level Three, and immediately signed on for formal training in child care. Their success has been important in helping every-one involved in the centre's adult education programme to raise their sights, and make sure they do not underestimate what parents want to, and can, achieve.

In the second year, the local TEC provided money to help get more courses going, and in September new classes and groups started. A 'new women' group, offering assertiveness training and career advice, a well woman group, and the English as a second language course, all started in the newly furnished room for adult groups. The TEC money will also help to provide the high quality creche that Chris Catanach sees as essential to any adult education the centre promotes.

Networks

Netherton Park is a family centre run to a very tight budget. However, it was impressive how much the nursery nurses who staff the centre had managed to take on and achieve in just nine months. A good quality base for a very wide range of work had been established very rapidly. One important reason that the centre has worked so well is that it set out to be a collaborative venture. The networks involved go well beyond the funding partnership. The centre has rapidly provided a convenient and productive focus to help different agencies offer new services for local families. It has built on established professional networks, and is developing new ones.

In late 1996, Chris Catanach was instrumental in setting up regular meetings for a group of local professionals from different services working with young children. They were planning to get together four to six times a year, to make sure there was good coordination between them. Most important, there has been a lot of consultation and collaboration between the centre and its users. The services provided are ones parents and other users have said they wanted. One of the challenges the centre may face in the future may be to persuade its founding partners to adapt their carefully negotiated 20-year agreement to make the most of new opportunities to meet new needs of families as they emerge.

Box 4.2   Netherton Park – summary

Strengths
- cooperation between local authority education and social services and voluntary sector on capital and running costs and management.
- Big range of education and care services.
- Excellent integration of special needs and family support with a local authority nursery school.
- Development of adult groups, some in association with local community college.
- Cultivation and development of local networks of different professionals dealing with families.
- Remarkable progress made in first year.

But
- So far no formal arrangements to offer health services at the centre.

Table 5.1   Greengables, Edinburgh

Services for children	Services for parents and other adults	Links with other professionals	Funding and management
Nursery school with full- and part-time places.	Wide range of groups and classes, some leading to Scotvec certification.	Social worker and community education worker on staff.	Funded by City Council Education Department and Urban Aid grant.
Extended day care.	Parenting groups.	Community medical officer visits regularly.	Non-executive advisory committee with parent, council, and local community representatives.
Holiday schemes for under fives and five to 12-year-olds.	Career advice.	Career adviser visits regularly.	
Creche.	Base for project for families of drug-users.	Base for social workers to work with families.	
Parent and baby and parent and toddler groups.		Speech therapist visits.	
Library.			
After school music group for primary children.			

5.   Greengables, Edinburgh

Introduction

'My main aim is that when a family comes here, we offer help in every possible way. We can provide education for the children in a flexible way, with our extended day. We offer recreation and education for parents. With our multi-disciplinary staff we can support and counsel parents when appropriate, and help them to move on', says Jeannette Scholes, head of Greengables.

Greengables in Edinburgh is a nursery school that just grew. There was no master plan at the start, no great vision. Everything that happened came from the school doing its best to meet the needs of its particular group of parents and children. The nursery school opened in 1975, on the edge of Edinburgh, where the concrete blocks of the Craigmillar and Niddrie estates housed many families living in considerable poverty and stress. The Craigmillar area has changed a bit since those days. Some of the nastier blocks near the school have been knocked down, and replaced by modern lower-density housing. There is now some private housing.

The area seems to generate self-help initiatives. The Craigmillar Festival Society started 30 years ago to run an arts festival, and now provides a wide range of services for local people. There is a local community-run centre fairly near the school with a café and various activities. But there is still plenty of poverty and stress, along with the problems drugs cause in several families – this is part of 'Trainspotting' country.

The school was purpose-built, with a big open plan space designed for 60 children, a smaller room for small group activities, a big grassy play area overlooking open countryside, a staffroom, head's office and kitchen, and a small room for parents. From the beginning, the aim was to involve parents as much as possible in the nursery. Several parents, feeling welcome, started to stay for long periods in the parents room. Soon it was bulging with babies, toddlers and buggies.

Since the parents were there, the staff thought they should offer something more than warmth and company and coffee. From the early days, there were parent and toddler groups. Gradually staff and parents started other groups, such as art and crafts sessions, and discussions about children. The activities were based on what parents said they wanted. The trouble was that there was still very little space and no extra staff. Everything offered to parents meant time away from the children. The head taught full-time. The staff not only organised activities for parents, but looked after their babies and toddlers while the parents took part.

In the late 1980s, Lothian Education Authority launched an 'open nursery' project, offering extended hours for some children of working or needy parents. It invited bids from schools wanting to house the pilot project. Greengables won the contract. The project brought more staff, in particular a home link teacher, a social worker attached to the school, and a teacher to free the head from teaching for half the day. The social worker and home link teacher soon showed the value to parents of their particular skills. But there was still no extra space for group activities, or for one-to-one work.

At this point Jeannette Scholes, who had been head for most of the school's life, and Kate Frame, the very experienced home link teacher, decided to go for broke. They applied to the Urban Aid fund for a whole new building and four extra members of staff, to house and expand the nursery's community activities. Soon afterwards, the social worker left, and the post became part of a general job freeze. Parents wrote pleading letters to the local authority, saying how much they had benefited from her work, but with no result. 'You can't keep making do, you have to move on', said Kate Frame. 'We worked out what we needed to take things a stage further. We needed a creche facility, extra rooms, a specialist community education worker, a social worker.'

They persuaded an architect working locally to design the building on a 'no win, no fee' basis, and sent off the bid. After initial surprise at this dramatic action, the Lothian authorities gave them solid backing. They won a grant of £330,000 for a new building, and £82,000 a year for four years to pay for new staff and running costs. The new building officially opened in April 1993.

'The new building'

They have never found a suitable name to describe the new project: 'family centre' has stigmatised social services connotations, and nothing else seemed quite right. Staff seem to refer to it as 'the new building'. It is a sizeable and attractive pavilion. A big central space has comfortable chairs, and parents can drop in at any time. There are two rooms used for groups and activities, one set out with tables as a classroom, and the other more informal with comfortable chairs. There's a smaller room, used for one-to-one sessions, and an open office for the home link teacher, social worker and community education worker. A well-equipped creche, run by two nursery nurses is in one corner, with doors to a good outdoor play space. There's a kitchen, used for cooking classes, general coffee making, and for parents to prepare buns and sandwiches for a weekly 'café'.

On the way in, there are a reception desk and pay phone. The Urban Aid grant pays the salaries of a community education worker, two nursery nurses in the creche, and the part-time receptionist/secretary. Social services provided a social worker, based in the new building, to work with families alongside the nursery's home link teacher. It makes an effective multi-agency team to meet the customers' wide-ranging needs. The most unusual resource in the building is a 'Snoezelen room', with soft mats and cushions and special equipment to provide relaxing scents and sound and light effects. It's used as a soft play area, by some of the adult classes to promote relaxation, and by nursery staff to calm down children when necessary. Locals can book in for private relaxation.

The building houses a big range of activities (see Table 5.2). All the classes seem open and welcoming to newcomers. When I was there a basic education class had two new students, who had settled down to work quickly. One of them turned up the next day to join a group that produces the Greengables newsletter. Christine McKechnie, the Greengables community education worker, evaluates every class, discussing how it went with participants. Aromatherapy is always very popular, easily filling three sessions a week. The class includes relaxation techniques and baby massage – excellent for mother-baby relations. Reflexology is another popular option. The aromatherapy and reflexology tutors both also offer free one-to-one sessions for individuals.

Many of the adult classes are geared in some way to the needs and interests of children. 'I go to sewing to make clothes for my own wee girl', said a mother. The cookery classes focus on low-cost, healthy family food. Cookery students say things like: 'We make things we normally wouldn't buy, and certainly wouldn't eat. Like spinach pancakes – they were green, it put you off, but when you tasted them they were lovely'. They comment that home-made pizzas and burgers are 'much cheaper and tastier than bought ones'. On my visit, the staff were also piloting a class for parents and children together. The tutor set out tables for making 'potty pizzas', 'silly sandwiches', and 'tempting tastes', letting children make and sample healthy low-sugar food. They loved it. Beforehand, the parents had a short session on nutrition, and the effects of poor diet on children's health as adults.

Several of the classes lead to Scottish vocational (Scotvec) qualifications, accrediting parents' learning and skills, and giving them the confidence to move on to courses elsewhere. Scotvec courses have included cooking, fabric skills, computer classes in a computer bus that comes every week from a local college, and a bricklaying course that enabled

Table 5.2 Free classes and courses at Greengables

Summer 1996

Monday	Tuesday	Wednesday	Thursday	Friday
Aromatherapy (Three different classes) Behaviour group Adult basic education Cookery (£1 charge for materials – take food away) Music for primary children	Cross-stitch Aerobics First Aid Greengables Gazette Reflexology Sewing (and Scotvec fabric skills)	Cross-stitch Adult Guidance (one to one sessions) Toddlers and Toy Library Talking about sex (Answering children's questions, women's health)	New options and choices Babies' play Computer bus Step aerobics Cookery (Charge as Monday. Possible Scotvec certificate)	Sewing Drugs project drop-in

parents to make raised flower beds and ornamental paths for the play area. It is easy for parents and carers to go to the classes, since the creche is in full swing all day. The two nursery nurses who run it are often helped by young people on training schemes at the college. Parents pay 25p a session for the creche, and can book places in advance.

A gimlet-eyed accountant might question the need for so many courses attached to a nursery, when there are other bases for adult education not far away. But many parents just would not go to classes further away. 'We used to try to take people up to courses only ten minutes away, but they said it was too difficult to get there' said Jeannette Scholes. When parents are coming to the nursery twice a day anyway to bring and collect their children, when there are staff they know well, and an excellent creche to care for their under-threes, people who are most unlikely to take advantage of opportunities elsewhere seem very receptive to education, advice and support at Greengables.

Young, first-time parents, isolated newcomers to the area, and parents who themselves have had special educational needs, can all benefit. I talked to two quite difficult-looking parents who had gradually been drawn into taking part in all kinds of groups: sewing, basic education, 'talking about sex' where 'we talk about how to tell children where babies come from'. 'It's fantastic, it's so local, and they don't force things on you', said one of them. Guidance is available for parents who want to move on to jobs or further education. They can book one-to-one advice sessions with a career adviser who comes in once a week, or go to the group that discusses 'options and choices'.

Christine McKechnie wants to use the premises to enrich after-school opportunities for primary school children. At the time of my visit, a music class run by two students from the local music college had just started. An appeal in the local paper for unwanted instruments had brought in a piano, recorders, a clarinet and violins for children to use. There are also one-off events. A man from the local Credit Union came in when I was there to explain how the locally run save-and-borrow scheme works. On the next day a group of parents was off on a day of challenging outward bound-type activities.

Amid all this activity, the social worker and home link teacher can make easy contact with parents. Together, they run popular 'behaviour groups', discussing how to manage tantrums, bedtimes, eating, and the other normal dilemmas of parents. The parents decide what topics they want to tackle. If appropriate, staff arrange for specialists such as the school medical officer to come in to answer their questions. Each group goes on a residential weekend with Kate Frame and Mary Gremson, the social worker, where they can try out new strategies with their children in enjoyable surroundings. There is no charge – the Greengables User's Committee applied to an Urban Aid Small Projects fund, and won a grant that covers the £240 needed for a weekend for five families.

Kate Frame has started a group for parents and babies, where parents watch the babies play with interesting everyday objects and materials and discuss how they learn from play and investigation. She also runs a weekly parent and toddler groups, and a toy library. The other part of her job is to visit parents and young children in their homes, offering practical support and knowledge about children's development. Families ask for these visits, or they may be referred by social workers, heath visitors and nursery staff. Numbers needing visits have gone down since so much became available at Greengables: in the summer of 1996 only four families were being visited.

A users' committee sets ground rules and discusses new ventures. Two members of the committee also sit on the main advisory committee (see *Finance and management*, below). The building is also occasionally used by other professionals. It provides a child-friendly place for local social workers to work with parents and children. After 2.30 on Friday afternoons, when the Greengables staff have their weekly meeting, a local project uses the new building for a drop-in to support families of drug-users.

Holiday schemes

Both the new building and the nursery provide holiday play schemes for children of working parents. In the new building the community educa-tion worker runs a scheme for five- to twelve-year-olds. The two nursery nurses who run the creche take turns to help, and volunteers also get involved. After experimenting with a bigger scheme, the staff decided that about 13 to 15 was the right number to offer children a positive and educational experience, as well as giving them a good time.

In the main nursery building, the home link teacher and one of the nursery nurses run a scheme mainly for the children who have extended day places (see below). Both schemes take children, and often their fami-lies, out and about a good deal. The holiday provision can't take all the nursery children who might benefit. But the social worker is also on hand, working with a few families whose children have particular needs, visiting them and helping to organise outings and activities for them.

The nursery

The main Greengables nursery is divided into two classes. One class has 20 places for children who stay for both morning and afternoon nursery sessions and lunch, and a further 10 places for children who can stay from eight to six. In practice, different children often take up the early morning and later afternoon places.

The other class has 30 places, and children come part-time for morn-ing or afternoon sessions. There is enormous pressure on the full-time and extended day places, and the lunch places, but extensive local provi-sion of nursery education means that parents who want part-time places can usually get them.

In the early morning the extended day children come in and quietly settle down to nursery activities. After school, the staff make sure that children who stay late have a change of tempo: quiet games or some-times a video, or a walk out into the country, as well as tea. The full-time and extended day places are earmarked for parents at work or college, and children of families under stress. The head, who knows the families very well after 20 years in the job – 'I started off very naive, and believed everything I was told' she says – makes the decisions about who gets the places.

The day before a child starts in either class, two members of staff visit the home to explain nursery procedures, get the parent and child to start filling in some baseline 'what I can do' information for a profile, and generally make sure the child sees familiar faces when s/he comes the next day. Some children come in with considerable behavioural and other problems. A supply nursery nurse, on her first Monday at Greengables, told me she was surprised by how difficult the children were. By Tuesday, she was equally struck by how quickly they had settled down to constructive activities. 'The staff are very skilful at managing behaviour – I'm not sure they realise how good they are' said a highly experienced teacher, previously a tutor on a nursery nurse training course, who was filling in for a teacher on a six months absence.

Good communication between staff is particularly important at Greengables. The two teachers and the team of nursery nurses in the full-time class work in shifts. Two part-time teachers share the other class, one taking the morning group and one the afternoon group. In the big outside play space, the children from the two classes merge. Both classes keep open loose-leaf folders on a shelf, with general plans for the day, and strategies to extend the work and interests of one or two particular children. In the full-time nursery the two shifts note down particular observations and happenings, such as brief details of a fight between two children. There is also a diary column, with administrative information, such as when children are being picked up, and by whom.

Staff in each class have a daily meeting to share observations and plan the next day's work. They draw up a planning sheet for the next day, with columns for the source, process, context and content of the planned work for the day, and a brief evaluation of how it went. So on a day I was there, the main source in one class was 'planting and growing'. There was a particular focus for two girls, to meet 'Danielle's interest in words and Kay's interest in letters'. A column showed which staff will do what, another noted the contexts where the children's interest could be developed (for example making egg and cress sandwiches for the snack).

On the wing, while they work and talk with the children, the nursery staff make brief notes about children's achievements and behaviour. The staff use the observations to extend children's skills, and later on distil them into a more formal profile. Staff often write the notes on sticky labels that go straight into the appropriate section of a profile form with sections on different curriculum areas. They note things like 'Language has improved by leaps and bounds – he said 'That machine's no working, it's broken' (filed under literacy: talking); or 'Knows sequence of numbers up to 10' (maths and science), or 'Knew that Samantha was holding the book upside down' (literacy: writing) or 'very reluctant to share toys – wanted the three diggers for himself' (personal and social development).

All these build into a profile, which ends with recommendations for progress. The profile is discussed with parents, and sent on to primary schools. It is interesting to compare the final profile with the collections of scribbled notes by staff. Between them, the staff build up a surprisingly clear and multi-faceted picture of the child's work in the nursery, and the teachers successfully condense the observations into the final profile. Each child also has a more personal album, with photographs of them taking part in nursery activities, drawings and their comments, as recorded by a worker ('My drawings have really come on, everyone can see it's a big monster') and coils of string to show children's height at different times.

Curriculum and planning

Staff meet at the end of each day to discuss their observations of individual children and plan the following day's activities. On Fridays (when local primary schools shut for the afternoon) the nursery children leave at 2.30 and there are no Greengables-run adult activities, so that all the staff can meet for longer-term communication and development. Workers take it in turns to look after the extended day children during this meeting.

In the first Greengables development plan, which ran from 1993 to 1996, a main priority was developing the work in the new building. Priorities for the nursery included policies for behaviour management and curriculum planning. The policies that resulted are very practical. The behaviour policy is based on valuing and praising children, and has succinct advice: never go to a child having a tantrum; after an incident always go to the hurt child first; remember that punishment only stops behaviour, it does not teach children what to do. The planning policy sets out criteria for themes and ideas introduced by the staff. Is the idea relevant to the child? Does it build on existing knowledge? Does it relate to the children's experience? Does it meet their developmental needs?

The nursery has been part of a wider focus on literacy, involving the whole local pyramid of schools, from nursery to secondary. It has developed a short equal opportunities policy (about to be revised) at the request of the local authority. Staff say they always tried to ensure the curriculum was multicultural: 'It's good for educating parents as well as children'.

Involving parents in the nursery

There are regular coffee mornings for parents every term, and 'fun evenings' about twice a year when parents are invited to come and try out nursery activities for themselves, giving staff a chance to explain the educational purpose of the activities in an informal way. There's plenty of evidence of the parents' commitment to giving practical help. A parent made low gates at the entrance of one of the classes. When vandals broke the windows of the new building early on, and they had to be boarded up until steel shutters arrived, parents painted pictures to brighten up the boarding. When the shutters finally arrived the pictures were cut out and used to decorate the nursery doors. The big outside play area has attractive raised flower beds and a winding path to a wild area, still being developed – all done by parents who worked with a bricklaying tutor from a local college. 'I always fancied myself as a brickie, but I'd never have travelled elsewhere to learn how to build', said a mother.

As well as the informal involvement, parents meet with nursery staff twice a year to discuss their children's progress and to go through their profile at the end of the year. The nursery also runs a library every Wednesday, where parents can talk about books and take them out for their children. The staff are good at spotting children's special needs and family problems, and with the social worker and home link teacher on the premises, and good links with other professionals such as the speech therapist, they can immediately offer appropriate help and support. 'When a head and staff are teaching full time you can't get so close to families: there is no time' says Jeannette Scholes.

Staffing and staff development

The staff consists of six teachers, including the head, senior teacher and home link teacher, two of them part-time, and nine nursery nurses, one of them part-time, as well as the social worker, community education worker and part-time receptionist/secretary. All the teachers and nursery nurses are on education contracts, with 12 weeks holiday a year. However, the home link teacher and three of the nursery nurses take holidays entirely or partly in term time, so that they can run the holiday schemes. The social worker, community education worker and receptionist are on different contracts, with three or four weeks holiday. This causes few tensions: 'It doesn't bother me. I knew the terms and conditions when I took the job', says Christine McKechnie.

The three professionals based in the new building all have their own professional support and development networks. Until local government reorganisation broke Lothian into smaller authorities in 1996, all the home link teachers in the region met regularly, as did the local community education workers. The social worker has a line manager in the local social work team. All these links mean that joint enterprises are easier to develop. Community education workers ran events across the whole area for Adult Learning Week, and Kate Frame and the local primary school home link teacher were planning a joint exhibition to inform parents about holiday play activities.

The nursery school on its own has a very small earmarked budget for in-service training: it gets £120 for each teacher. There is nothing in the budget for nursery nurses. However the Urban Aid grant brought an extra £1500 a year for training. As well as training for the nursery staff, the budget has allowed the secretary/receptionist, who is in the front line when talking to parents and other users, to have some counselling and assertiveness training ('Have you learnt to say No?', asked the head when she returned) as well as computer training. Greengables is itself a popular training centre for other colleges, with student nursery nurses, teachers, social workers and community education workers all coming regularly on placements.

Links with other professionals

All the staff say that it is enormously valuable having a social worker on the premises, adding a new dimension to the services the nursery can offer to parents. She is able to support families in many ways, and link them in to other support services and community organisations. At first there were worries that the title would put parents off, and various euphemisms such as 'family worker' were considered and rejected. When the staff finally decided to call a social worker a social worker, it did not seem to faze the parents in the least. The great strength of a social work base in the nursery is that the work is preventive. 'Mary gets involved in families before they are at crisis point, and need their own social worker', said Jeannette Scholes.

There were high hopes at the beginning of the open nursery project that there would be a system of regular visits from a health visitor. Health visitors did come in to run some courses for parents, on safety in the home, or giving up smoking. But regular links have not increased, as originally hoped, partly because of all the recent changes that have affected the health visiting service. Instead, Greengables staff contact health visitors when they see a need. However, the Community Medical Officer makes monthly visits.

The local speech therapist has made regular visits. At one point the nursery had 21 children needing speech therapy, and some of them were missing out when their parents found it difficult to take them up to the clinic. So the speech therapist agreed to run sessions at Greengables. The arrangement had the advantage that a nursery nurse could sit in on the sessions, and help make sure that parents and other nursery staff understood the suggested strategies. Recently the number of these sessions has had to be cut back: demands from other schools have meant that the speech therapist has to spread herself more thinly. The educational psychologist comes when needed, and has joined staff sessions when strategies for specific children were being discussed.

Finance and management

Greengables does not have a delegated budget. Edinburgh City Council (which took over from Lothian in 1996), manages the nursery school finances. The head is responsible for the £20,000 or so a year spent on supplies and services. She is also responsible for the Urban Aid grant of £82,000 a year for salaries and running costs attached to the new building.

There is no governing body. Instead the centre has an advisory committee, which meets once a term. Members include all the agencies concerned with children and families. There are managers and a councillor from the Education Department, a social services manager and the district nursing officer, the assessor for the Urban Aid project, the local adult education organiser, a community representative from the Craigmillar Festival Society, and three parent representatives. The head reports to the committee, and receives support and guidance from them. They have no executive role but the range of advice and support they can offer is a great strength to the project.

Future prospects

At the time of my visit, Greengables was entering a period of some uncertainty. The initial three-year Urban Aid grant runs out in May 1997. The grant pays for the community education worker and tutors, the creche, and the part-time secretary and receptionist, and it provides money for running costs, training and development. The evaluation of the project's first three years (and earlier evaluation of the work of the extended nursery) has been very favourable, and the hope was that the project might be given a three-year continuation under Urban Aid.

Failing that, the future will depend on whether the new Edinburgh City Council will be able to provide funds to sustain the work, or whether funds can be raised elsewhere. Edinburgh was facing £10 million cuts in the current financial year, and expected further cuts in the future. Social services would want to continue to pay for a social worker at Greengables: they value the preventive work that such outreach makes possible. 'It's a good use of £25,000', said David Wilkie, who manages social services' provision for children in South East Edinburgh. 'The only way of freeing a few social workers from the child protection juggernaut is to attach them to this kind of project.' He says that Greengables can help parents at an early, preventive stage, and 'in as unpatronising a way as is possible'. But at a time when social services may well have to close one of their own children's centres in the area, a further contribution to Greengables, perhaps to fund the creche, which is an essential part of the service, is unlikely.

The Education Department is also 'very happy with the whole structure', according to Wendy Dignam, senior adviser. 'It is expensive, and difficult to replicate, but it has proved itself time and time again', she said. 'A lot has happened because there are people from different disciplines, with different ways of working, who are really in tune with that community. They have thought things through, built up expertise, and implemented new ventures very carefully. There's a teaching and learning component in everything they do, and the results benefit whole families'. She believed that that the council would find ways to make sure that the work continued.

The project certainly deserves long-term support. Greengables' organic growth from nursery school to wide-ranging family and community education centre is a remarkable success story. The parents who use the centre, with its new facilities and opportunities, go further: almost every one I talked to used the word 'fantastic'. 'The big disappointment is that it is only likely to be able to continue as a 'special' project', said David Wilkie. 'It shouldn't be "special". Every school ought to be able to provide child care for parents who need to return to work, and to have good facilities for parents to come in and help along their children's education and their own.'

Box 5.2   Greengables – summary

Strengths
- High quality extended day nursery education, creche and holiday care.
- Range of adult education and support.
- Services grown from community needs.
- Staff from different professional backgrounds.
- Long-serving and entrepreneurial senior staff, in tune with the community.

But
- Uncertainty about long-term funding of adult education and support.
- Little regular involvement of health visitors.

Table 6.1   Robinswood Family Centre, Gloucester

Services for children and parents	Services for adults	Links with outside professionals	Funding and management
Drop in for 0–5-year-olds. Under threes group and three-plus group.	Various classes – basic English, pre-GCSE and GCSE English, German, computer literacy, First Aid, Keep Fit, Book-keeping, Calligraphy. (Most classes run in cooperation with local Neighbourhood Project with creche at centre.)	Speech therapist once a week.	Funding from County Education Department.
Nursery class – up to five part-time sessions a week.		Health visitor – fortnightly baby clinic, visits to Open House once a month.	Linked primary school gives premises and services free, funds teacher and nursery assistant for nursery class.
Weekly speech and language group.		Social services family support worker, monthly visits to Open House.	City Council gives small grant for holiday play scheme.
Baby clinic.	Introduction to Child Care course.		Centre coordinator manges all staff.
Holiday play schemes for 0–6-year-olds (with carer) and 3–6-year-olds (on their own).	Careers Guidance.		Management Committee with school, LEA, and community representatives and parents.
Creche.			

6. Robinswood Family Centre, Gloucester

Introduction

Robinswood Family Centre shows what can happen when people working for different agencies collaborate successfully, within a clear local authority framework, suppressing inter-professional irritations and territorial imperatives, and working on the simple basis that they are all serving the same families in the same neighbourhood.

In early 1970s, just after the Education Secretary, Margaret Thatcher, had published a White Paper promising a huge expansion of part-time nursery education, Gloucester built two large 60-place nursery units attached to primary schools, and created a third in a redundant building. But government money for new nurseries never materialised, and they were left empty. So they appointed a teacher in each of the schools with a brief to set up some services for pre-school children and their parents. Local playgroups were more than happy to use the buildings, and the teachers started other groups and projects. The new buildings were called 'family centres'.

By the early 1980s, the general lack of pre-school provision was gaining a higher political profile in the county. The response was to set up six new family centres, run by the Education Department, in areas of high social need. The Matson estate in south Gloucester was a strong candidate. There were high levels of deprivation – and desolation – on the estate. 'It had a terrible name, and was very run down. There was litter and scrap everywhere. Most of the street lamps were broken' says Terry Allen, the long-serving head of Robinswood, one of the primary schools on the estate.

He and his chair of governors, a powerful local councillor, campaigned for a centre on the estate. The timing was right – the junior and infant schools on the same site were about to be merged, creating some space in the school. The Robinswood Family Centre opened in 1986. The needs were evident: the 1991 census showed that in Matson one third of households were headed by single parents, one third had someone suffering long-term ill health, the unemployment rate was 20 per cent, and much higher for young people, and fewer than 50 per cent of households owned a car.

The family centres were each given a teacher coordinator, a further 0.7 of a teacher, and a nursery nurse. The aim was to offer educational groups for children and opportunities for adult education and training. By 1996, Gloucestershire had started 15 family centres, all working to the same brief (see Box 6.1), but able to vary their provision to meet their particular community's needs. For example, one, with a large number of Asian families, provides adult language teaching and groups that suit them. Another, with many traveller families, has to run particularly flexible services.

Box 6.1   Extracts from the Gloucestershire Education Family Centre's Service Charter

What we do

We provide
- Quality educational experiences for the Under 5s and their families
- Education for adults
- Training placements for a variety of students
- Information and links with other agencies

Standards of service you can expect

- Our staff are friendly and welcoming
- We provide safe play areas for the children
- We create close links with the local community and its school
- We try to provide what you say you need
- We believe that all members of the public, children and staff, are entitled to equal respect and service
- We provide information about a range of services of interest to young families and can suggest sources of specialist help to those in need
- We are open for at least 190 school days a year (some of us provide holiday and out of hours activities too).

Help us to help you

- We use questionnaires to find out what our users think of our service
- We value everyone's help and support, especially on our helpers' rotas and our management groups
- We will listen to what you have to say

At Robinswood, good relationships between the school, family centre and education authority might well have foundered when Robinswood became the first primary school to take grant-maintained (GM) status in 1992. Instead, they seem to have gone from strength to strength. It probably helped that the centre's coordinator, Siri Heaven, and nursery nurse, Val Knight, had both been members of the school staff.

The school was able to use the comparatively generous capital funding available to GM schools to build a new nursery class, due to open at the end of 1996. In a staggeringly sensible arrangement, the school in effect handed over the management of its new nursery class, and its staff, to the family centre. The coordinator of the family centre also manages the admissions to the school. So in September 1996 the family centre was able to offer five day a week part-time nursery schooling to 68 three and four-year-olds, as well as various sessions for babies and younger children and their parents, and a range of educational opportunities for adults.

The building

The new nursery building was not quite finished at the time of my visit in September 1996. (The school provided a classroom to take the over-spill so that the new nursery children could come in as planned.) The new building will link to the centre's existing large play space, converted from a former classroom. The centre has a big entrance room – built when the family centre opened – with room both for buggies and indoor climbing equipment. The central area has more play space and equipment and an alcove for small groups to meet. Leading off it there is an office, a small room reserved for older children with a computer and other special equipment, and the small infant school staffroom, now furnished with a comfortable sofa and chairs.

An old store room has been turned into a small kitchen where parents and staff make themselves drinks and snacks. It has a washing machine that can be used by parents in times of need. Rebuilding and renovating has provided good toilets for children and adults, and a shower and baby-changing room. Through the kitchen, a door leads out to the outdoor play space, which has been transformed from a flat muddy grass patch to a good area for physical and imaginative play, with new climbing equipment and slides on a mound, and a superb tarmac bike track with speed limits, road signs, a zebra crossing and a petrol pump.

The planning and design of the outdoor area were the work of a mother who had taken basic education classes and a child care course at the family centre. She had compiled an impressive folder with reports of interviews with local officials responsible for parks and playgrounds, details of insurance requirements, designs for the playground and quotations for equipment and building work.

Groups for children

The family centre offers a range of groups for children from birth to five. Mothers have been known to drop in on the way back from hospital to introduce their new-born baby to the staff (and a member of staff always knits a jacket for the baby). But most parents come when their babies become mobile. The groups are very friendly and flexible. If parents are attending a class at the centre, or down the road at a nearby community adult education centre, there is no separate creche – instead, their children join in with whatever is going on, and a student, parent or member of staff is detailed to keep an eye on them.

All the services for children are virtually free. Parents are asked to pay 40p a session so that the children can be provided with healthy drinks and snacks. For the two 'open house' sessions each week, when anyone with a pre-school child can come along, the charge is just 30p. At those open sessions, parents and children play with all the excellent equipment, which is all kept on open shelves at child level. Siri Heaven, the coordinator, and Val Knight make themselves available to talk to parents, in private when necessary.

There is one session a week for under threes and their carers, where babies and toddlers can play and get used to being in a group, sitting round a table to have a snack or joining in a song or a story. It's a very happy occasion until leaving time comes, when there are often tears and protests. Parents can withdraw during the session for a drink, so children become used to being left on their own at the centre.

Another weekly session, run by a teacher, caters for rising threes. Parents and carers stay with the children. When children become three, they move on to the twice-weekly 'three plus' group, where they stay on their own with a teacher, nursery assistant and a rota of parents. The sessions offer the pre-nursery children play and activities on High/Scope lines (see *Curriculum planning and development*, below).

The new nursery classes can take up to 75 children for up to five half day sessions a week. Parents are asked to come in and help six times each term. There is no possibility of offering parents all day care – 'It's not what we are about', said Siri Heaven. On my visit, the nursery groups had 68 children. Gloucestershire's policy is that all children start primary school at the beginning of the school year in which they will be five, so most nursery children will stay for one year. Children in the nursery groups do not have to come for five sessions a week. Some attend other groups catering specifically for special needs once or twice a week; others have parents who prefer fewer sessions.

Admission criteria for the nursery groups have been agreed with the school. The order of priority is children with special needs living in Matson and neighbouring Abbeydale; children with siblings in the school; other children living in Matson and Abbeydale; and finally children with special needs from further afield referred by GPs, health visitors, social services or educational psychologists. All families who live locally are made welcome in all the groups, whatever children's stage of development or special needs. 'You can see the relief in parents eyes when we say they can leave three-year-olds who are still in nappies' said a member of staff. Parents told me they liked the mix of people you get when a centre is open to a whole neighbourhood.

Since the great majority of children go on to Robinswood primary school, a child living locally can move easily through the centre and on to school in a familiar environment with familiar routines. The reception teachers visit the nursery groups, the older nursery children take part in school events, and there is good communication between nursery and reception teachers. Terry Allen, the school's head teacher says: 'Our children start school with well developed pre-school skills. They know how to hold a pen and use a paintbrush, and how to take themselves to the toilet. Most can dress themselves. They know their numbers and colours, and many have started to read. They are used to being part of a group, and sharing. They come into our reception classes and take off'.

Even though all the staff are on education contracts, with school holidays, they raise funds each year to run a summer holiday play scheme. There are open house sessions and sessions for three- to six-year-olds, where children can be left on their own. The staff would like it to run five days a week for four weeks, but usually the funds available from the City Council and elsewhere only cover a more limited service, with six sessions a week.

Support for parents

Parents told me how helpful it had been to have the informal advice and support available to parents in all the groups. 'They're always here with an ear to listen and a bit of advice', said one mother. 'Siri is fantastic. If you have any problem of a personal nature, she is wonderful' said another, who had burst into tears at an open house when suffering postnatal depression, and been offered immediate support. A mother whose young child became seriously distressed at the time of the Rosemary West trial – their family church was very near 25 Cromwell Street – told me that the staff had been a tremendous help. They had encouraged her to make contact with a child psychologist who had offered reassurance and advice at an early stage.

At the under-threes group, a mother had brought a two year old with as yet undiagnosed problems. He had a mental age of nine months, and his sleeplessness and behaviour (not least his passion for sloshing water around, and his tendency to break things) made life very difficult at home. She said the family centre had kept her going, making the child welcome at the groups, and giving her a break to attend a keep fit class at the centre, while a qualified member of staff looked after the child. 'Here, everyone is welcome', she said. 'In other parent and toddler groups, parents whisper and discriminate if you bring a child with special needs, even though the other *children* aren't in the least bothered.'

Other professionals come in to the centre to offer support and advice in an informal and accessible way. A community family worker, paid by social services, comes to an open house session once a month. She has also run groups for parents, where they can discuss the everyday problems of bringing up young children. A health visitor has a clinic at the centre every fortnight, and visits the under threes group once a month. A speech therapist runs a weekly 75 minute session for a small group of children with language delay or difficulties. A member of staff helps with the session, which means the work feeds back into the regular groups.

Some parents (such as the mother who designed the playground) have done a Parent and Toddler Association Introduction to Childcare course. On my visit a Parent Link group, led by the community link worker, was about to start, as was a first aid class. 'It's a pretty comprehensive service, when you think about it', said a parent. 'There's even a hairdresser who comes once a month, and cuts our hair for £1.'

Opportunities for adults

The family centre offers a variety of classes and groups for adults, either on the premises or at neighbourhood centres nearby. Until September 1996, the local further education college, Gloscat, ran many of the classes. Tutors from the college had run a range of classes, including basic education, pre-GCSE and GCSE English, French, basic computer literacy and information technology and book-keeping. There were also New Beginnings classes, offering career and educational guidance along with confidence-building, assertiveness training and an introduction to computers.

However in the summer of 1996 Gloscat reviewed the provision, and decided that numbers in the groups were not high enough – they had previously provided tutors for groups of eight or ten, but now stipulated 13.5 as a minimum. (Other Gloucestershire FE colleges, such as the one in Cirencester, have taken a different view, and continue to support classes in their local family centres.) The change was particularly galling, since the arrangement had seemed to work very well. The staff at the centre could encourage and cajole parents who were nervous about going back to education in any form. The college reached a clientele who would not otherwise use their services. 'We worked very hard to motivate people, and if the service is taken away they may not bother again' said a member of the Robinswood staff.

Mothers and childminders said they could never attend classes in the city: 'It's two buses, a £1.40 fare, someone to mind the children, and an hour added on before you start the class' said one mother. At Robins-wood, they could leave the children with staff they knew. The college tutors found the centre was a rewarding place to work, and a number of women moved on to access courses and further education. A mother who had taken the Wordpower basic education course said it had also helped her children. The course had included ideas for activities that parents and children could do together to help the children develop their reading and writing.

To some extent, another local resource has filled the gap left by Gloscat – the lively and successful Matson Neighbourhood Project. The project uses money raised from the European Social Fund, business sponsorship, and other sources to run a variety of activities – a community shop, careers advice and training, computer classes and other adult education. Parents can leave their children at the family centre while they go to classes nearby. Several of the courses are free for those on benefit or working 16 hours a week or less. Fe Clarke, a worker at the neighbourhood project, regularly visits the centre. 'The centre is an excellent focal point for promoting the courses and finding out what people want', she said. 'It's the place in the community where people feel most comfortable and confident'.

The centre itself organises some groups. The Gloscat languages tutor made a private arrangement for a group of parents and minders who had got a long way with French and were now starting German – partly because a new start with a new language would make it easier for newcomers to join. However she could not offer Gloscat's concessionary rates for people on benefit. She said it was important to offer classes that could accommodate flexibly to people's different goals and rates of progress: 'It's not always right to aim directly at a qualification.'

A teacher at the primary school with experience of aerobics runs a keep fit class once a week, while Siri Heaven takes her class – another example of the easy collaboration between school and family centre. 'We have found that the three key blocks to people taking up training and education opportunities are lack of confidence, lack of knowledge about the options and providers, and a high level of caring responsibilities', said Fe Clarke. 'The family centre removes all three barriers for people with young children.'

Curriculum planning and development

Five years ago, the family centre introduced the High/Scope approach to its work with older children. The centre is arranged with all equipment on accessible shelves, clearly labelled, in labelled areas – books, home corner, construction toys, sand and water, art and craft and so on. In the three plus and nursery groups, children start the day by planning what they will do, and the day ends with a session where they review what they have done in their key worker groups. At some stage in the session, they also have a small group time, when the staff introduce activities linked to a theme. When I was there, early in the first term for the nursery children, the themes were 'getting to know you' and colours.

Staff meet once a week at the end of the day to plan the week ahead, deciding who will do what in the small group time. (Red was the colour of the week when I was there, and there were plans for the children to cook plum crumble.) They also spent some time planning how to deploy the students doing placements at the centre (see *Staffing, staff development and training,* below).

At the end of each three-plus and nursery session, the staff meet briefly to review the activities and progress of individual children. They make sure all children are regularly mentioned, collect observations, and plan future needs and suitable activities. They use the notes and observations at these sessions to build records of children's progress, which are discussed at meetings with parents.

The staff also prepare a record of achievement and pre-school profile for each child. They and the school's reception class teachers discussed what kind of profile would be practical and useful. They drew up a set of statements about aspects of children's development: relations with peers and adults; independence and decision making; disposition ('confident', 'usually cheerful', 'apprehensive', 'prone to temper tantrums'); language and literacy; mathematical skills; and self-help skills. Staff ring the statements that apply to the child, add brief comments, and discuss the results with parents, incorporating their comments.

More curriculum development has resulted from the centre's involvement in the national Effective Early Learning project. After a lot of self-review, structured observation of children, and questionnaires and discussions with parents, the staff found that while quality and curriculum coverage were generally good, there were areas that needed monitoring. One was maths, science and technology, Another other was language – some children were doing less talking, both to adults and to each other, during their free choice play than staff had thought.

They also found that while parents were generally delighted with the centre's services, they did not really grasp the educational aims and objectives of the centre's work with children. Even the management committee was a bit hazy about the centre's educational aspects. The 1996 action plan addressed all these issues. It stated clearly how progress would be demonstrated (for example by structured observation and tracking of children, and interviews and questionnaires for adults), what resources would need to be deployed, who was responsible for progress, and the timescale for action.

Staffing, staff development and training

The staff consists of the coordinator, who teaches four nursery sessions a week, as well as taking part in open house and under three groups, two teachers, a nursery nurse and a nursery assistant, and an administrator who is paid to work for eight hours a week (and volunteers a great deal more time). Although the primary school pays one teacher and the nursery assistant, who work mainly with the nursery groups, the staff are managed, and work together, flexibly as one unit. All staff have staff development interviews every year. The coordinator's supervisor is the Gloucestershire Education Officer responsible for under fives.

There are the normal five in-service training days each year. Two of the days are joint sessions with staff in other Gloucestershire family centres. The staff can also bid to attend other courses from the LEA budget for training. Some multi-agency training is available – for example, one member of staff went on a child protection course alongside health and social workers and police officers.

Robinswood is a regular and popular practical training base for students. On my visit, there were eight students on the premises (too many, but Siri Heaven had capitulated to the pleas of a local tutor). Some were just doing a few days or weeks' placement, others would be there four days a week for the whole year. They were on BTEC, NVQ and NNEB courses, and there were also some Project 2000 nursing students. Social work students use the centre to undertake child observations. I met a student's BTEC tutor who said family centres provided excellent placements, giving students a lot of contact with parents as well as with children.

Organising the students' supervision and development is a big load on a small staff, particularly at the beginning of the school year. One of the students on my visit clearly appreciated their work. 'Compared with my last placement, the staff here are really motivated and they give us a structured programme, telling us what we're going to do and why', he said.

Funding and management

The family centre is managed by the Education Department. The school pays for two of the staff and 50 of the new nursery places, but delegates management to the centre's coordinator. Social Services pay for the visits of the community family worker, and the health authority pays the health visitor, and shares the cost of the speech therapist with the Education Department. The school provides the site and premises rent-free, and charges administrative expenses, such as photo-copying, at cost. The LEA pays running costs, such as rates, heating and cleaning. The school and the LEA cover all staff salaries between them. That leaves the centre with £2070 for resources and other administrative costs.

When the school went grant-maintained, a management committee was set up for the family centre. It includes staff and parent representatives, one of the school governors, representatives from the Matson Neighbourhood Project and the Education Department, the health visitor and community family worker, and people representing other local interests. The committee meets once a term to receive the coordinator's report and monitor progress. 'We make sure that the centre runs for the benefit of the children', said a parent member of the committee.

In 1995 Robinswood Family Centre qualified for an Investors in People award. 'It made us put down what we were doing on paper. All the staff knew our policies and could justify our aims and objectives, but it made us look at communication and record-keeping, keep minutes, and draw up or tidy up policies. At the time it all seemed too much, but it has saved us time in the end', said Siri Heaven. As a result of the work, the centre now has a very crisp set of policies for its pre-nursery sessions and nursery; for equal opportunities; for health and safety (with a clear checklist of safety measures staff must observe); a brief behaviour policy; guidelines for parents when they work at the centre; and a policy and detailed checklist for the induction of new staff, students and volunteers working at the centre.

A striking feature of the management of Robinswood is the way it seems to allow for easy inter-agency cooperation. 'We're all in the same business, providing for local children and families. There's no place for empire builders and ego trips', said Terry Allen, the school's head teacher. There are also good links with other agencies in the neighbourhood, not just the Matson Neighbourhood project, but also the local churches and the youth service. They combine to campaign for the interests of the community. For example, together they lent power to a successful campaign to save the local library from closure, and have it refurbished.

Outcomes

With the family centre as a focal point for this cooperation, both children's and families' needs can be picked up quickly, and good support is offered. Terry Allen is in no doubt that the family centre's work affects not only children's readiness for school, but their behaviour and happiness. The school used to need a special unit for children with behaviour problems, he says. 'We don't any more, and the family centre must be one important factor. We're seeing a general increase in behaviour problems and developmental delay – but the family centre offsets that.

'It's somewhere where parents under stress, frequently young, frequently single, can find support and an outlet for their worries from a very early stage. It's a godsend if you're bringing up a family in a small flat, perhaps with difficult neighbours. It gives children what they need: space, and stimulation, and a chance to use their energy.' A mother of a two year old put it more simply. 'Children and parents both need this sort of a place. Children learn to play with each other. If I didn't have this place, I'd be belting him at the end of the day.'

Box 6.2   Robinswood – summary

Strengths
- Open access for children and carers from birth to school.
- Range of opportunities for adults.
- Participation of health and social services.
- Unusual sharing of responsibility, staff and facilities with grant-maintained school.
- Promotion and use of local networks.
- Use of external tools for development – Effective Early Learning project, High/Scope, Investors in People.
- Very effective local networks.

But
- No day care.
- Successful cooperation from local FE college withdrawn.

Table 7.1   The Dorothy Gardner Centre, London

Services for children	Services for parents and carers	Links with other professionals, and services offered	Funding and management
Drop-in for children 0-5 and their carers. Day care and education for one to two and a half-year-olds. 52-place nursery for two and a half to five-year-olds. Provision for lunch and extended day. Holiday play scheme. Integrated education for children with special needs – autism, Downs syndrome etc. (No wheelchairs possible). Speech therapist and educational psychologist regularly visit .	Drop-in open all year. Toy library. Workshops and discussion groups about young children's development and learning. Some adult education classes. Free creche for those attending workshops. Staff with counselling training. Course for local childminders, leading to NVQ.	Links with health visitors, physiotherapist, social workers, educational welfare officer etc. Good links with child protection team, family therapy unit, family centre, adult education centre. NVQ assessment and training centre for primary school assistants. Practical training base for social work, education and medical students.	£400K from Westminster City Council: 49% from Social Services, 51% from Education. Education lead department for management purposes. Funds raised from local trusts and charities for toy library, holiday play schemes. About £2000 raised from staff contributions to training courses, conferences etc. Management Council with no legal powers, but treated as a governing body. Responsible for delegated budget.

7. The Dorothy Gardner Centre, London

Introduction

The Dorothy Gardner Centre was one of the earliest of the combined nursery centres, opening in 1975. It was built and planned by a local charity, the Mulberry Trust, after advice from one of the most distinguished experts on child development of the time, Professor Jack Tizard. The Trust then handed the building over to the London Borough of Westminster, with a trust deed that ensured there should be no radical departure from the original vision. That vision was for a neighbourhood centre within pram-pushing distance for children and parents, giving them access to a wide range of services to support them in the upbringing and education of their young children.

At the start, the vision was partly blocked by administrative barriers. The head teacher of the nursery school and the officer in charge of the day nursery were managed by the former Inner London Education Authority and Westminster social services respectively. The coordinator was left with only the building and mothers and toddler club to manage. For the next 15 years flexibility and cooperation were very difficult to achieve. The two nurseries shared stock cupboards but not resources, a formula for territorial disputes. If one nursery was short of staff when the other had staff available to fill in, there was no provision for sensible cooperation.

All that changed in 1992. Bernadette Duffy, then deputy head of the 'education' nursery, became Head, and Liz Reavey the deputy in the 'social services' nursery, became Deputy Head of the centre. Both wanted to offer genuinely integrated care, and genuinely flexible services for children under five and their parents. Under Bernadette Duffy's lively, democratic and open-minded leadership, the Tizard vision became a reality for local residents. The centre has been highly praised by visiting professionals: its latest accolade came in a glowing OFSTED inspection report in late 1996, which concluded: 'The Dorothy Gardner Nursery Centre is a beacon of excellent practice. Children from birth to five and their parents and carers derive tremendous benefit from this integrated social services and education provision'.

The centre's focus is squarely on children's early education. (See Box 7.1) 'All our work starts from education and learning' said Bernadette Duffy. The flexible hours, and provision of breakfast and tea for some children, is provided to make sure children have access to education. Westminster's policy does not offer any priority for parents in full-time work or education.

Box 7.1   Aims of the Dorothy Gardner Centre

'To provide a fully-integrated, high-quality education and care service for children under five who live in the catchment area.

To achieve this we need to ensure that:
- Each child knows they are valued and their background (culture, race, religion) is understood, respected and reflected in the Centre. From this basis each child can maintain and develop a confident and positive self-image which is the foundation of a happy and successful life.
- We recognise that children are part of a family. Parents have a unique insight into their child's abilities. By working in partnership with them we can provide the best opportunities for each child and support for the parent/family role . . .
- Each child has access to a broad, balanced and relevant curriculum which matches their age, abilities and needs.
- As a multi-disciplinary team we draw on a wide range of expertise, some based on the centre and some outside. Each individual has a particular role and responsibilities that enhance the work of the centre.'

The neighbourhood

The families using the centre represent an unusually cosmopolitan mix. In 1995 29 per cent of families originally came from the Caribbean, and another 29 per cent were from the UK. Nine per cent originally came from Morocco, and six per cent from Pakistan. Ireland, Nigeria and Portugal all produced five per cent, North America four per cent, while others originally came from the Philippines, Iran, Italy, Sweden and Poland. They live in a mixture of council housing and large Victorian family houses, some of which were taken over and 'gentrified' by well-off professional families in the 1980s. So the children's socio-economic backgrounds are as mixed as their national and ethnic origins.

The whole centre used to be open all year round. But budget cuts meant that in 1996 two members of staff had to be made redundant and the nursery could only be fully open in term time. The drop-in and toy library continued through the holidays. Nursery children sponsored by social services were still eligible to come in the holidays, and others could come if enough volunteer parents and carers could be recruited. However, energetic fund-raising secured enough money to keep the centre open for all children in the holidays in 1997.

Building and services

The centre replaced two houses on a corner site, and had to be designed as a clever piece of infill. It is on four levels. The nursery takes up the two lowest levels, and is built round a small play area. This has been broken up into different spaces, all tiny, but offering different environments: a central play space, with equipment for climbing and sliding, a roofed over section (which was being used as a flower market for plants grown in the nursery on my visit), a jungly area, and a quiet area with benches and a small climbing tree with a rope ladder.

The nursery has a room for seven young children, aged one to two and a half, who are looked after by two key workers. It is furnished in a domestic style, with a big sofa, and the children are often taken out on visits to the shops and park and nearby canal, as well as going out into the main nursery and playground. The main nursery has a separate room for music and dance, and an old windowless store room has been painted and filled with floor cushions, so children have a quiet place to retreat from all the activity. The remaining open space has been partitioned to form distinct areas that cover different aspects of the curriculum.

The main entrance is up some steps from the street, on the floor above the nursery (the building is impossible for wheelchairs). It has a small reception area with comfortable seats for parents, and information about the centre and its policies for people to read and take away. Between the reception and the nursery, there is space for a toy library, staffed by parents and open two mornings and two afternoons each week. Parents pay £1 for life membership, and 20p per borrowing. There is an excellent stock of toys and materials for all stages, from baby toys, through wooden train sets and dressing up clothes, to packs of books and tapes and crayons for four-year-olds.

A dining room for children who stay to lunch or tea doubles as a meeting room. Upstairs, much of the space, including the corridors, is devoted to a drop-in, which runs four days a week for any parents or carers with young children. Staff and visitors have to pick their way round toddlers and adults, absorbed in play, to get to the two offices. A big room at the end is used as a community meeting room, a classroom, and a play area for the drop-in, with a ball pool and big soft blocks.

The staff room doubles as a room for small discussion groups and adult classes. It all demands a very intensive use of limited space, and in the centre's action plan for 1996, staff were investigating possibilities for acquiring new premises nearby so they could provide more services and benefit a wider community.

The drop-in

The Dorothy Gardner curriculum starts from the time parents and carers bring their babies in to the drop-in. It has its own big room, and spills out into the corridors and the community room. The emphasis on multicultural variety is noticeable from the start. There are pictures of children with their parents: 'Gabi's daddy comes from Columbia and Gabi's mummy comes from Mexico. Gabi is learning Spanish and English.' In the home corner, the basket of play bread has nan and pitta bread as well as traditional English loaves and buns.

The drop-in is open to all comers living in Westminster, and about 90 families use it, mainly for babies and under-threes. Up to 25 children can come in each session, and morning regulars told me they took care to get there by 9.15 to make sure of a place. A father with a 20 month old son said; 'He *begs* me to come'. People bring in their friends and neighbours. Neighbours who are concerned about a child sometimes persuade the parent to come to the drop-in. It's a way of doing something without taking the big step of formally reporting worries or suspicions.

The drop-in is laid out with sand and water, areas for imaginative play, books, glueing and sticking, painting and so on. Adults play alongside their children, chatting to them and to each other. One or two members of staff are always on hand to play with children and talk to parents. There is a corner for babies, equipped with 'treasure baskets': collections of interesting objects most people could have at home. For example there are plastic bottle shakers full of rice and beans, and a basket of metal objects such as keys and chains.

One of the workers runs a weekly discussion group on topics parents have suggested, often concerning children's behaviour, feeding and sleeping problems, or practical activities such as making mobiles for young children. The drop in is also used as a creche for parents going to classes at the centre. On Fridays, a group of local childminders takes over the drop-in space. In 1996 some of them had just embarked on an NVQ course, based at the centre. Liz Reavey, the deputy head of the centre, had raised funds for the course from a charity. Minders can also use the regular sessions. 'This place is *beautiful*', said one, who came most days.

Staff try to give parents the support they want: first-time parents like ideas and information about children: experienced ones often respond to opportunities to branch out into further education and training for themselves. Liz Reavey is a trained counsellor and the centre used to offer counselling sessions for parents, but found a very small number wanted long-term support that the staff could not offer. However she now prepares parents to go on for more extensive help at the local Family Service Unit – a service that can be difficult to refer yourself to without encouragement. 'There is no stigma when the whole neighbourhood uses the centre, and it is perceived to be about children's education' said Bernadette Duffy.

Under threes curriculum

The curriculum for under-threes is very carefully planned. Much of it is based on the work of Elinor Goldschmeid, a well-known expert on 'heuristic play' for babies and toddlers (Goldschmeid and Jackson, 1994, Goldschmeid, 1987, 1994). She was a key advisor when the centre was being set up, and has worked with the staff. Babies who can sit up are offered sensory play, based on the treasure baskets. Once children get more mobile, and in to what the workers call the 'what can I do with things' stage, more everyday materials are made available. At that stage children can spend an hour or more exploring the properties of paper and tubes and ribbons and containers. Parents see how children learn from exploring everyday objects at home.

I watched an older baby for about 10 minutes as, with the utmost concentration, she tested what happened when she dropped different things down a tube. She tried some jingly metal things, then some corks, and gradually, and with evident interest and excitement, worked out where the objects had gone. 'It's important they're given every chance to concentrate on what interests them – in some early years settings, a lot is adult-led' said Liz Reavey. A mother told me: 'They all have big eyes at Dorothy Gardner, there's so much for them to do.' Parents and staff talk about the ideas behind the curriculum and resources both one to one and in the discussion groups and monthly curriculum workshops.

The nursery

The nursery has places for 52 children, plus seven children under two and a half. One third of the children are referred by social services, and the rest come from the local community (see Box 7.2). Most children come part-time, since demand for places is very heavy, but 23 children were staying all day, and up to 28 can stay for lunch. Eight children can stay for tea, if they or their parents need an extended day.

The nursery has a staff of eight, three teachers and five 'early years educators'. There is also a 'float' worker who covers staff absences, undertakes observations of children, and helps with trips and outings. At the time of my visit, they had just completely reorganised the nursery. Instead of providing a separate room for two- to three-year-olds, the nursery had been opened up for all but those under two and a half. Resources had been grouped in different curriculum areas – a large

---

Box 7.2   Dorothy Gardner Centre Admissions Policy

Education places

The catchment area is eight surrounding streets.

First priority: children with professionally identified social, educational or medical needs.

Second priority: children who live nearest to the centre.

Social services places

First priority: children whose names are on the child protection register or at risk; children admitted as part of a planned programme of work with the family; children who are subject to a court order, or where provision of day care would remove the need for court action.

Second priority: children with physical or intellectual disability; children whose development is delayed or impaired.

Third priority: families who need professional help caring for their child because of physical or mental health problems; seriously poor living conditions; relationship difficulties which may impair the child's development; other serious stress or pressures.

Fourth priority: families receiving family credit or income support.

---

creative and imaginative area, a maths area, a literacy area with books, a big sofa, and tapes and headphones, an area for science and technology, and a separate room for music. All resources are accessible to children, so they can pursue their own interests. Each member of staff spends a week in one of the areas, working with children to extend their ideas, and observing them.

The Dorothy Gardner nursery is a particularly lively and stimulating place to visit. Children draw you into their games and use you as a resource when they need a passing adult. It's very welcoming for parents – a pregnant mother was resting in nursery's reception area, which has comfortable chairs for adults; a father was absorbed in building a large castle with blocks, ostensibly with his son.

The curriculum is based on the Westminster early years guidelines, *Great Expectations* (Westminster, 1996), which Dorothy Gardner staff were closely involved in developing. Some activities are adult-led, and that is made clear to the children: the staff say 'I want you to...' not 'Would you like to ...?' On my visit there were some very enthusiastic groups in the new music room, listening to music, trying out different kinds of walking to fit, and then doing some aerobics with Priya Deva, the Senior Teacher.

Each member of staff is a key worker for about nine children, and the staff plan their work in pairs, with one teacher and one early years educator. The two are given time on Fridays for detailed planning of activities to meet the needs of individual children the next week, and of the knowledge and skills the activities will promote. The nursery staff plan activities that fit children's current interests. For example, at the time of my visit, an interest in St George had somehow led to an interest in hospitals, which had broadened into a focus on service industries in the creative and imaginative area.

The staff keep running notes of their observations during the day, with a particular focus on a selected group of 'target' children, but also noting interesting activities and conversations of other children. At the end of the day the nursery staff meet to share their observations, and plan the next session. For example, the music and aerobics session had provided a lot of information about individual children's coordination, their ability to follow instructions, their sensitivity to interpreting music, and their knowledge of how the body works: 'James knew that the heart pumps blood round the body.'

Some of the plans develop from regular consultation and 'conferencing' with children. The nursery reorganisation was in part based on older children's perceptions of the nursery. They were very polite, saying things like: 'The adults put out what they think children like but it may not be what we really want', and asking if perhaps one or two tables and spaces might be left for their own projects and intentions. They had decided views about the difference between work and play in the nursery: 'If you do a picture for your Mum that's play; if you do it for your key worker, that's work.'

The nursery sessions have a clear routine. For the first half hour children do what they want, so staff are free to talk to parents. Staff then work with groups of children for half an hour, before stepping back to observe children's activities, and unobtrusively extend and talk about what they are doing. The children briefly meet in key worker groups, then move on to language groups, based on their age and stage of development. The youngest have stories with prompts and support, such as felt boards and props. The oldest and most advanced do more formal work on reading and writing.

In 1996, the OFSTED inspectors found that teaching by all the educators was very good throughout the nursery, and excellent in parts. They commented that 'teachers' awareness of child development, their close knowledge of each child, and their ability to present the subject matter to children in a way that excites interest and sustains involvement, is of an extremely high order.' They found that children's attainment in all areas of the curriculum was beyond national expectations.

Special needs

The nursery, with its steps and different levels, is not suitable for physically disabled children, but it takes many other children with special needs. At the time of my visit there were two autistic children and one Downs syndrome child, who came with their own assistants. There was also a child with cystic fibrosis. About a quarter to a third of the other children have identified special needs, mostly language or developmental delay. Dorothy Gardner, with its drop-in for very young children, is a good place to pick up needs early, and make sure parents have good support and information.

The staff have time for real continuing partnership with parents to meet the children's needs, in a way that staffing and time constraints make impossible later on, when the parents are dealing with overstretched primary schools and psychologists. For example the parents of an autistic child found out about the Lovas programme, a highly structured scheme that they thought might help their child. The nursery staff and the educational psychologists were doubtful, but agreed to give it a try. It was time-consuming and expensive, but it proved very successful. Westminster's education department has now funded a worker to extend the programme to other autistic children.

Parent involvement and adult groups

Parents are closely involved in the work and planning of the nursery and drop-in. On the one-to-one level, the nursery key workers make themselves available for prolonged chat and discussion with parents at the beginning of each session. Parents meet their key worker more formally once a term to discuss their children's records and progress.

Dorothy Gardner has a clear and detailed set of centre policies, covering all the areas of the curriculum as well as general issues such as planning and equal opportunities. Parents are involved in the policy-making, and there can be lively debates in well-attended curriculum workshops that take place one Friday each month. For example, the policy on spiritual and moral education involved a lot of argument about whether boys should be allowed to go in for 'superhero' play based on Power Rangers and the like. Parents of boys argued that they needed to act out those interests, and a decision was taken to allow the play, but work to minimise any violent aspects. The workshops look at both practical matters, such as choosing primary schools, and discussing theories behind the early years curriculum.

The centre runs popular assertiveness training sessions. On my visit, a very lively group of women was telling (with some glee) how they had successfully applied what they had learnt, handling stroppy children at bedtime, and difficult mothers in law, without getting aggressive or angry. One woman had screwed up her courage to go to an aerobics class for the first time. It was a very enjoyable session, and seemed very effective.

A language and literacy group for speakers of other languages is always well attended – eight or nine people were going in 1996. Other groups, such as keep fit, start as and when people request them and a tutor or organiser can be found. The centre has run a group for fathers who had positively chosen to be the main carers of their children – but had then been rather daunted by the reality. Most classes are charged at the Westminster adult education rates, which include concessions for people on low incomes. A creche is provided free.

Holiday play scheme

Before the cuts, the centre had enough staff to run a free holiday play scheme. After some discussion, the management committee decided it should be for under fives only, in line with the centre's 'core business'. Children, and some parents, went on a lot of outings, to places like Richmond Park and to the seaside. After the staff cuts, the centre has managed to keep the play scheme going on a different basis, with grants from charities and more direct involvement of parents helping to run it.

Staffing, staff development and planning

The centre has a senior management team of three: the head, the deputy, and the senior teacher. Bernadette Duffy, the head, is a teacher by origin, but worked in a day nursery before joining the Gardner nursery in 1986. She says her experience of working in a social services setting was very valuable: at the time social services had more sophisticated policies for staff development and supervision than schools. Liz Reavey, the deputy, had NNEB training, and had worked in social services day nurseries.

In the nursery, teachers and early years educators all have the same core responsibilities, but the teachers have extra responsibilities for leadership curriculum, and management. Each teacher takes responsibility for one area of the curriculum, and leads training sessions for the other workers. Teachers have higher pay and longer holidays than nursery nurses. The early years educators accept that trained graduates should earn more, though the size of the gap occasionally rankles. But the nursery nurses are better paid than they would be in schools and day nurseries – they earn about £15,000 a year, with up to six and a half weeks' holiday each year.

There is a strong culture of professional review, leading to new responsibilities for staff, along with opportunities for professional development and training. All staff have a member of the senior management team as 'mentor', and meet with her at least once a term. They agree targets, and discuss training opportunities. Once a year, the mentor observes the member of staff at work, after agreeing a focus for the observation. For example one member of staff wanted to concentrate on her conversations with children: she had found it difficult to get them talking. The observation showed that she was asking a lot of direct questions, rather than taking a back seat and responding to the children's interests.

The centre closes at 3pm for one Monday each month, so there can be an extended staff meeting, as well as closing for the usual five training days each year. All staff are encouraged to go in for further training. They have taken degrees in social science or early years education, and diplomas in early childhood studies. A nursery nurse has taken an access course as preparation for teacher training. Others have trained as counsellors. The centre pays for the training and offers paid study leave for courses that need it.

In 1995, the staff, parents and management committee drew up a five year development plan, with an action plan for the first year. They audited what they had already achieved under several headings: curriculum, parents, community, management, staff, premises and resources. They then identified what aspects of the centre they wished to preserve, and what they wanted to develop in future. A one year action plan assigned time scales and responsibilities for the immediate tasks.

The centre is well used for placements of students training for a range of professions concerned with children – social workers, teachers, nursery nurses and health professionals. The local teaching hospital sends medical students, partly to show them that children can often do things in comfortable and familiar surroundings when they would fail to perform in the consulting room. In 1996, the centre had recently become an NVQ accredited training centre, and childminders and primary school assistants were training there, with the centre's staff running sessions on curriculum and child development.

Links with other professionals

The centre has a link health visitor, who comes in regularly on request – though her participation has not been helped by the new system where health visitors are based in GP practices, instead of having a local patch. There are also very close links with other local services for families: the family services unit, a family therapy unit at the local hospital, the child development team and a social services family centre. The Dorothy

Gardner staff can act as a bridge, encouraging parents to use the other services, which are often more daunting to approach.

A speech therapist visits the centre every Monday afternoon, and an educational psychologist visits the centre three times a term, and will help if there is an urgent need in between visits. The local adult education centre is an important resource for adult groups, providing tutors for some of the courses run from the centre.

Funding and management

The high quality services offered at Dorothy Gardner do not come cheap. The centre is jointly funded by Westminster's education and social services departments, and in 1996 the total grant was £400,000. A nursery place at the centre costs about £4,000 – compared to about £2,400 for a place in an ordinary nursery class attached to a school. 'You have to be very clear what you're offering that is worth the extra funding' said Bernadette Duffy. She argues that the centre's role in training, and staff development for others, its importance as a model (managing hundreds of visitors is an extra responsibility on staff) and its input into Westminster curriculum and professional development, provide some answers.

There is also the preventive aspect. Picking up special needs at an early stage means that early intervention and support can make it possible for more children to stay in mainstream education and can save thousands of pounds, with special education costing up to £25,000 a year. When parents become involved in their children's learning and curriculum at the earliest possible stage – preferably when the children are babies – it can have important effects later on. 'With the best will in the world, a primary teacher with a class of 30 or more can't do nearly as much to develop parents' skills as educators. Our parents are used to going in and asking: "How can I support him at home?", says Bernadette Duffy.

When Westminster Social Services needed to find cuts in 1996, it planned to take £140,000 out of the Dorothy Gardner budget. Within half a day, the parents had mobilised a massive campaign against the cuts (luckily, the staff were all tied up in a meeting that day, so there was no hint of collusion). The campaign wasn't only conducted by the more educated professional parents, though their skills and contacts helped. Families who had been on the social services priority lists also wrote letters to councillors and told them and the press what a difference Dorothy Gardner had made to their and their children's lives. The cut was reduced to £50,000.

Grants from trusts and charities bring in some extras, such as toys for the toy library and £1000 for outings. The staff's contribution to training and conferences elsewhere brings in about £2000 each year. After the cuts, Dorothy Gardner staff and parents are well aware that expansion and development will have to come from fund raising.

The management of the budget is fully delegated. There is a Management Committee, with all key interests represented on it – parents, staff, community representatives, representatives from the founding Mulberry Trust, local councillors, and officers from Westminster Education and Social services. The committee meets twice a term to advise and support the management, oversee the budget, and 'makes sure we stick to our core business'.

Outcomes

In 1993 Westminster commissioned an independent inspection of Dorothy Gardner, using the new OFSTED framework. The two experienced former HM Inspectors concluded: 'Such a quality pre-school provision is unique in Westminster, and rarely to be found elsewhere in the country...The centre has achieved that rare balance between a clearly defined curriculum and the opportunity for the individual development of children within it...[It is] a most stimulating environment in which to work and play.' The judgement still stands, and the 1996 OFSTED report, under a different inspection framework, was if anything more enthusiastic.

Dorothy Gardner, with its clearly stated 'core business' of the education of children under five from babies upwards, in partnership with parents and carers, is an outstanding example of what a well-led and well-resourced early education centre can achieve. It benefits from the fact that its area of Westminster has generous nursery provision, and most children stay in the nursery until the term in which they are five.

Its local, genuinely 'comprehensive' intake of children and families means that the staff develop very high expectations of what young children can achieve, and parents and children benefit from the presence of families from wide range of backgrounds and cultures. Partnership with parents and carers builds from the time children are babies, and the centre has been unusually successful at drawing parents into quite detailed aspects of children's learning and the nursery curriculum.

As an open access, very local, neighbourhood centre, Dorothy Gardner attracts many people in need of support who would not necessarily come to the attention of other support services. The success of the resulting preventive work has not been measured – but it is noticeable that families referred to the centre for child protection reasons do not usually need any social services support for their younger children. It may have taken 15 years to realise Jack Tizard's vision of a neighbourhood centre to meet the educational and social needs of young children and their families – but Dorothy Gardner today shows what a powerful force such a centre can be in children's and parents' lives.

Box 7.3   The Dorothy Gardner Centre – summary

Strengths
- Excellent leadership, promoting good teamwork and planning.
- Very high-quality education for children from birth to five.
- Rich curriculum for children under three.
- Classes and groups for parents.
- Parent involvement in curriculum and policy-making.
- High parent commitment.
- Some all-day care.
- Good links with other local professionals and services.
- Good support for children with special needs and their parents.
- Intensive use of all available space.

But
- Holiday services suffered from funding cuts.

Table 8.1   Chase Children's Centre, Hampshire

Services for children and parents	Links with other professionals	Funding and management
Two-hour sessions for children with parents.	Health authority provides special needs leader, social services other special needs staff.	Jointly funded by Education (£31,000), Social Services (£16,000) and Health (one part-time salary).
Sessions for children with special needs and their parents.	Speech therapist, physiotherapist, occupational therapist and community medical officer visit regularly.	Three-year service level agreement between the three services and the school governors.
Some sessions in school holidays.		
Outreach to other neighbourhood parent and child groups: runs toy library for one outside group.	Member of local early years forum: runs joint projects with them and with a local charity.	Delegated budget, through Education Department.
Home visiting.	Good links with adjacent primary school.	Executive management committee with all funders represented, as well as parents and fund-raising Friends of Chase.
Groups on parenting.		
English class for speakers of other languages.		
Information about other local groups and facilities.		

8. Chase Children's Centre, Hampshire

Introduction

Bordon in Hampshire is an army garrison town in the middle of beautiful, and mainly very expensive, countryside. As well as mobile army families, the late 1980s saw rapid building of small starter homes, occupied by young parents who were cut off from the support of their extended families. There is also a caravan site, and some short-term and emergency accommodation, as well as council housing estates. Bordon County infants school was built in 1980 in the middle of regulation issue blocks of army maisonettes and houses. But round the corner from the school, you suddenly come across a large, warm and inviting Norwegian log cabin, standing out from its surroundings – the Chase Children's Centre.

The centre grew out of two separate projects. One was a pre-school group, started by the infant school's head teacher, Sarah Broadbent. She had become increasingly concerned about the lack of support and encouragement for families with pre-school children, and the missed opportunities for some parents to help their children's development. The school did its best, with pre-school home visits and a strong philosophy of parent involvement, but it could not do much to help parents in the vital early years.

She started a 'pre-school partnership' group in 1985, and adult education funded a tutor to help run a weekly session for parents and young children. Roger Haddock, the Area Education Officer visited the group, and found it chimed well with his own wish to do more to support families with young children and get them involved in education long before school age. So he offered the school a full-time teacher to work with families and younger children, provided they came up with a suitable project. Eileen Torbet, who had worked in special schools and playgroups as well as mainstream primaries, got the job. Gradually the groups and services grew, with home visiting and sessions for parents and children playing together.

Meanwhile Pat Lambert, the Principal Medical Officer for Child Health in the area, had become very aware of the fragmentary support received by parents of babies and toddlers with special needs. By the time they got in to special provision, many opportunities for early intervention had been lost. She also wanted to bring parents of children with special needs together as soon as possible to share difficulties and strategies, and to have more integrated provision where they could mix and play with other local families.

Lambert got money from the health authority and social services for staffing a special needs group in the Bordon area, but could not find suitable premises. Roger Haddock brought her together with Sarah Broadbent, whose flourishing pre-school scheme had just moved to the junior school next door because infant school numbers went up and there was no longer a spare classroom. Broadbent and Lambert discovered they had very similar aims, and the special needs group moved in to share the pre-school project's premises. Increasingly close contacts soon developed between staff and users of the two schemes.

When the junior school, too, was about to run out of space, fundraising began for a new building for a family centre on the school land. A local group called the Friends of Chase successfully set out to raise the £75,000 needed, and the log cabin was ready by 1990. The building opened in 1990. It is expensive to maintain – the wood has to be treated every two years. But after six years of heavy use, it is still spick and span and gleaming. There is a large, welcoming play space, with a few adult-level seats scattered around (though not in groups: the space is designed for adults and children to play together); an office, kitchen and toilets; a room (about to be extended) for small groups; and a covered veranda with steps down to a small, well-landscaped outdoor play area.

The Hampshire context

In the mid-1980s, Hampshire had very little mainstream nursery education. Some infant schools, such as Bordon, set up do-it-yourself pre-school groups, but most nursery provision was in the private and voluntary sectors. However, in the late 1980s, provision for the early years took on a much higher profile in the county. Spurred partly by the Children Act and partly by a strong impulse in the Education Department to do more, the council set up a joint subcommittee of the education and social services committees to look at policy to support young children and families.

The challenge was to expand and diversify provision at a time when new statutory responsibilities were multiplying, funds were contracting, and health, education, and social services were all undergoing considerable upheavals. Given the circumstances, Hampshire achieved a great deal. On the education side, it introduced a policy where all children started infant school in the September of the year of their fifth birthday. The policy was backed with new resources, classroom assistants, and

---

> ## Box 8.1   Aims of the Hampshire early years centres
>
> To provide:
> - carefully structured play-learning facilities for children;
> - assessment opportunities, support and appropriate therapy programmes for individual children;
> - advice and guidance for the parent or carer from qualified and experienced professionals in health, care and education;
> - opportunities for parents to learn together and to build ideas;
> - opportunities for parents to share and, through participation, to enjoy the development of their children.
>
> To act as:
> - a focus for early years work and development in the area;
> - a meeting, training and potential assessment centre for individuals and local groups;
> - a base for outreach work to the local community in facilities such as homes, playgroups, nurseries and schools.

in-service training, to try to make sure the youngest children had an appropriate curriculum and environment. Once under way, outside consultants were appointed to evaluate the results and make recommendations for improvements.

There were a few nursery schools and classes in needy areas. These provided conventional nursery education, but also became part of a planned network of early years multi-agency family centres to support parents with young children, giving priority to those with special needs. The aims of the early year centres are summarised in Box 8.1. By 1996 ten centres were up and running, all slightly different in origin and emphasis, but working towards the county's criteria. Six more were planned. Partnership with parents, the 'first educators' of children, was the watchword.

The Chase Centre, which had grown organically with support from both Education and Social Services, became one of the first such centres. It is run according to the Hampshire plan, under a service level agreement between the local health trust, Education, Social Services and the governing body of the primary school.

Groups

The core work at the Chase Centre takes place in ten half day sessions each week. The centre does not cater for children on their own, except in very rare cases where a family needs respite care for a few hours. Children come with their parents or carers for two structured hours of play and activities. The only charge is a suggested 25p per session for snacks and drinks. Four of the weekly groups are reserved for children with special needs. Five are open to all comers, and one is a mixed group with both special needs and mainstream children – a good stepping stone to full integration. One of the mainstream groups caters for all ages. The others divide roughly into children under and over three. There is no starting age: parents can and do bring their babies along.

The mainstream groups cater for up to 12 families each session, with two extra places available for mainstream children referred by outside professionals. The special needs groups are smaller and quieter, with up to ten families, so that staff can work more intensively with children and parents. When I was there 79 families were coming to the open groups each week, and there were 30 families in the special needs group.

There is some overlap between the groups. Some children who are referred to a special needs group for conditions such as speech or developmental delay can make rapid progress and catch up with their age group. Other children who come to mainstream groups turn out to have special needs, some of them serious. Children – or parents – with special needs take priority for admissions. The staff have discretion to let a family jump the queue, if they think early admission is necessary. The catchment area is the whole of East Hampshire, though most children come from within a ten mile radius. Social services pay transport costs for families with special needs.

The workers visit all families of children with special needs at home before the children start at a group. The leaders of mainstream groups make home visits when appropriate. Over the first few weeks at the centre, staff and parents fill in a sheet, noting what the child is good at, and what difficulties he or she may have. Parents mention a range of problems, from sleeping, eating and joining in with other children to more serious matters such as slow speech development. They identify areas where they think children need encouragement – work on number or colours; self-confidence; language development; behaviour problems. Then they and the staff agree a plan to tackle the difficulties at the centre and at home: for example 'Try just giving her what she wants to eat' or 'Allow him plenty of time to speak.'

The groups have a clear pattern of activities. Sessions start with free play and some special activities related to a curriculum theme. After an hour or so, music plays as a signal for children and parents to clear up, and they then go into the infant school hall for energetic songs and movement and group activities. They come back for a snack time, all sitting round a table (there is a quiet emphasis on behaviour and manners), and there is a session when all the parents share books with their children. The session often ends with singing games, rhymes or discussion. During the sessions you see the workers having long one-to-one chats –

and a lot of laughs – with parents. They talk about children, and also about parents' difficulties at home or with other agencies. You also see the staff unobtrusively modelling ways of encouraging and talking to children, and allowing them to do things for themselves, rather than the adults doing everything for them.

At the time of my visit, the centre was about to introduce the High/Scope curriculum, with its emphasis on children planning and reviewing their work, in all the groups. The staff had already introduced a review session for each group where children (with a lot of prompting) described their activities during the session. Eileen Torbet says: 'What interests me is turning out people – both adults and children – who can make decisions and choices. The important thing for children at this stage is how they cope with life, their self-esteem and feeling of self-responsibility'. She believes the High/Scope structure, and its emphasis on children undertaking real-life everyday activities, will promote this.

The parents who bring children to the centre can't praise it too highly: 'It's heaven', said one mother. Most children come for one session a week, and there is a long waiting list for places. Several parents also use playgroups for older children, where they can be left on their own. 'Both set-ups have their advantages, but when they're under three this is much better' said a mother. 'It feels right to be doing things with your child, and there are more adult workers here to do things with the children'. Another with an older child said: 'We can go home and carry on with ideas they've enjoyed here. Playgroups give you nothing to work on'. Staff say that some parents who come to look at the centre decide that its structured approach is not for them. If so, the staff can put them in touch with other local groups that might suit them better.

Parents of children with special needs or developmental delay seem in no doubt that the early support and intervention offered by the centre has made a huge difference to their child. 'Last year he hardly spoke, now he won't shut up. He might have had to go to a special school, but he's done really well after one-to-one sessions here', said one mother. The staff consider that one of the best indicators of the value of their work is the number of children who have come with special needs and gone on successfully to mainstream primary school. The very early support and intervention that the centre can offer also help children with more severe difficulties, and their parents, when special nursery provision only starts at the age of three.

All the parents are asked to keep diaries of their children's activities at the centre and, if they wish, at home. During every session, you see most parents settling down at some stage to write the diaries. 'It makes them look for positive things, and notice what their children are doing and learning' said a family worker. 'It's interesting looking back and seeing how he's come on', said a mother. The staff also keep records of children's progress, with notes under the main curriculum areas of language and literacy, maths, knowledge and understanding of the world, and creative, physical and personal and social development. There is a day book where staff write brief notes of what happened after every session: 'we need it for continuity between groups, and it helps us to note what's gone well.'

The staff choose curriculum themes as a base for the more structured work, and start every week by planning more detailed aims and activities for the week's groups. During my visit, the groups were all focusing on 'growing': children had planted seeds, and were now measuring their own height, and doing drawings and collages of their development since they were babies.

Multi-agency work

The centre is a base for a number of professionals who work with children with special needs. The Loddon Health Trust pays for the leader of the special needs group (who works 20 hours a week). The post was vacant when I visited, but a very experienced health visitor and college lecturer was soon to start in the post. A speech therapist visits the centre every Monday, and an occupational therapist and physiotherapist each visit once a month. The community medical officer also comes each month. These health professionals mainly work with the children with special needs and their parents – but they are also available to talk informally with other parents if they have particular worries. 'Here, we could get my daughter's ears checked through the doctor, and she can reassure you when you worry unnecessarily' said one mother.

The centre is open for 46 weeks of the year. In term time, it is in full swing with two sessions each day. It stays open two days a week for part of the holidays, so contact and support for families can be maintained, and the staff visit some families at home during the holidays. Other voluntary groups also use the premises in the holidays.

It is seen as an invaluable resource by professionals who find families needing support. It provides a social base for isolated newcomers to the area, and early support to prevent difficulties with children becoming real problems. The fact that it is open to all parents and children is seen as central: 'They know parents are there because they have a pre-school child, not because they have a problem', said a local professional.

Outreach

One important aim of the centre is to support other pre-school groups in the neighbourhood. At the time of my visit, workers from the Chase were directly involved in two other groups. One was an informal drop-in for parents and under fives in a community centre down the road. The group attracts large numbers of mothers, babies and toddlers, and one of the centre's family workers and a former parent were running a toy library there.

The toy library was an excellent service in itself, offering a big range of toys, some of them large and expensive such as ride-on cars, trampolines, and wooden train sets. It cost parents £1 a term to join, and 30-50p for each toy – and big items were delivered free. It is organised by a volunteer, who says that the Chase Centre 'saved my life'. When she moved in to the area she spoke very little English, had a bad stammer, and was very isolated and depressed with her three year old child. The toy library also gave a Chase family worker an opportunity to work alongside the regular leader, talking to parents, helping them with practical problems, and encouraging some of them to become more interested in their children's play and development.

Eileen Torbet herself was going each week to a new drop-in group on a very isolated housing estate in an otherwise well-heeled area a few miles from the centre. The group was a collaborative venture, started with an adult education tutor with support from the local under eights forum, and sharing equipment with Voices, a local charity that supports families in difficulties. She took along some of the centre's more specialised equipment, such as musical instruments, for children to play with, and she and the adult tutor spent the session playing with children and chatting to parents, often about their children's development, or about any other problems they wanted to discuss (one had brought in an official-looking letter in for deciphering).

Both outreach projects were very informal and unstructured, but it was clear that many parents valued the chance to talk about their children with a knowledgeable professional, and to find out more about educational activities that their children enjoyed. The Chase workers also go out and support families in their homes, if for some reason the groups on offer at the centre do not meet their needs.

Networking

As well as outreach, the Chase staff act as an information centre and switchboard. They are in touch with other groups, such as playgroups and mother and toddler groups, and can tell parents about other services they can use. 'We can act as a one-stop shop: we know where people and services are, and can put parents in touch with them' said Eileen Torbet. On occasion local voluntary groups have invited them in to advise them, or help them interview for a new leader. One of the family workers runs a 'Face to Face' group, that puts families who have just discovered their child has special needs in touch with families who have already experienced the feelings and challenges they are facing.

Eileen Torbet has been very active in helping to set up and maintain the flourishing local under-eights forum, and represents the forum at the county advisory meeting, which includes elected members. It is part of Hampshire policy to support a complete network of under eights forums, creating new ones where none exists. In the Bordon area, the forum has done a lot to develop the cohesion and voice of all the people working with young children and their families in the area. It has given them the courage to lobby county officers and members when necessary. It also provides a pool of people with different skills who can contribute to work with under eights in the area, and encourage new projects.

Staffing and staff development

The head of the centre and the special needs leader have year-round contracts. There is a leader of the open groups, who works for 22.5 weeks in term time, and, along with other family workers, is contracted to work for one week of the summer holidays. The three other family workers are paid social services rates, and work for 30, 15 and nine hours a week respectively. The work is clearly interesting enough to attract qualified and experienced staff: one of the family workers is a teacher, and another a nurse with good experience of working with disabled people and of residential care. 'It's the staff that make the centre', a parent said, and the variety of professional backgrounds and experience clearly strengthens the work.

Multi-agency funding and management also increase the amount of low-cost training available to staff, and the centre takes as much advantage of it as its slim training budget allows. The health authority runs useful practical courses in things like lifting and handling children; the Education Authority provides nursery training, and Social Services run courses on aspects such as child protection and listening skills. But Eileen Torbet says that there is still a shortage of appropriate training for work with early years, particularly under-threes.

Some of the workers have taken counselling courses, and others have done some work on post-natal depression. The links with the infant school are productive: staff sometimes go into the school to help in the reception and Year One classes, keeping them in touch with the next stage of children's education. High/Scope training has been a good spur for staff development and critical discussion. And as in many centres, the Effective Early Learning project run by Professor Chris Pascal at Worcester College of Higher Education has been a profitable source of review and development. It has involved a lot of observation of children, and evaluation of practice, with a particular emphasis on children's autonomy, the sensitivity of staff to their needs and intentions, and the stimulus offered. The staff drew up an action plan, focusing on maths and science in the curriculum, implemented it and then evaluated it.

The centre also acts as a training base for others in a small way. The head is an NVQ assessor, and supervises local classroom assistants and playgroup volunteers who want to work for NVQ qualifications, and the centre is used for placements for students on nursery nurse courses.

Adult education

Since the centre is only open in the daytime, and most of the staff work part-time, the scope for adult education on the premises is limited. In 1996, there was an English for speakers of other languages course for three parents, and a tutor was coming in once a week to run a family skills course. The staff would like to expand their work with adults. In September 1996 a group at the centre, run by health visitors, covered topics such as sleep, toilet training, first aid and behaviour management. The centre's staff looked after the children at one end of the building, while the parents met in a group at the other end.

Another new venture they were hoping to set up was an information technology course, run by a local college tutor who would bring in a set of laptops computers. The class would go ahead provided space in the infant school could be made available after school hours, with the centre used for a creche. All these courses are cheap to run if premises can be found. The local under eights forum is a good source of volunteer speakers, and runs its own parents' groups, and local colleges are keen to support outreach work.

Funding and management

The core running costs of the centre are met by the local health trust, which pays for the special needs leader (20 hours a week); the Education Department, which contributes £31,000 a year, mainly for salaries; and the Social Services Department, which contribute £16,000, covering the family workers in the special needs groups. The budget is delegated to the centre through the Education Department. After staff salaries, and a £1000 payment to the primary school's community budget to cover some of the running costs met by the school, such as caretaking, cleaning and consumables like paper, paint and glue, the centre is left with £3000 a year. This has to pay for staff travel costs – which are quite high, in a spread-out rural area – staff training; and most office equipment and costs.

The Friends of Chase brings together staff, parents, users and other supporters, and raises around £3000 a year. This is usually spent on extra equipment. In 1996 an army charity gave a grant for books to set up a pre-school lending library. The centre is affiliated to SCOPE – formerly the Spastics Society – which provides some management support and training. The charity was an early supporter of the centre, and in 1996 contributed to the extension of the small group room.

A service level agreement sets out the basis of the funding, operations and management of the centre. The partners are the school governors (since the centre is on their land), the County Education and Social Services Departments, the North Hampshire Health Commission, and the Loddon Health Trust. It was the first of such agreements set up by Hampshire for an early years centre, and will run for three years from 1995. It stipulates that the centre will provide structured play sessions, including sessions for special needs, and outreach to individual families and groups. It also sets out the contribution of the various parties: for example health will provide a clinical medical officer and therapists, and Social Services transport for children with special needs.

The head of centre is the line manager for all the staff (although the special needs leader also has a line manager in the health trust). She herself has the head of the infant school as line manager. There is an executive management committee, with all the partners to the service level agreement represented, along with two Chase parents. The committee is chaired by the chairperson of the Friends of Chase. All these arrangements are now typical of Hampshire early years centres, and give them some stability of funding and management.

Outcomes

Within its fairly limited resources and space, the Chase has been very successful, and a model for the new network of early years centres in Hampshire. The staff would like to expand further, running more adult education, introducing respite care for parents, and promoting after-school opportunities for primary children, but so far neither they nor or the infant school has the space and resources to do more.

Sarah Broadbent, the head of the infant school, believes that the pre-school work has helped parents to understand that they are the first and main educators of their children, and to share responsibility for their education with the school. 'If a child is unhappy or something goes wrong, the parents come in and we try to work on it together – it's about problem-solving not about blame.'

At a time when infant schools are reporting increasingly difficult and anti-social behaviour in young children, Bordon Infants had not recently had to refer any child to a psychologist for behaviour problems. Only one child in the school has needed a statement of special educational needs. Some of this is clearly down to the school's own policies – by no means all its pupils start at the Chase. But the pre-school work must also be a significant factor. Sarah Broadbent believes that it has affected the parenting culture of the whole area, generating positive attitudes that spread to families who have never used the centre.

Viv West, the area director of Social Services for Alton and Aldershot is equally positive about the effects of the Chase Centre. She says there has been a marked decline in the number of children in the Bordon area who need to be referred to the Social Services family resource centre. That centre deals with children with severe problems, who usually get referred at about the age of eight or nine.

She picked out several key reasons for the success of the children's centre. Families can be referred to it at a very early stage in the child's life, which means that children's needs can be diagnosed and met, in partnership with their families, at a vital stage in the child's development. The centre mitigates the isolation many parents face in rural areas, bringing parents together and helping to develop their confidence. The holistic approach means that the different professions dealing with children work together, rather than trying, sometimes ineffectively, to solve problems on their own. Finally, she says, it is very important that the centre is open to all comers, and its users are not stigmatised in any way.

Box 8.3   Chase Children's Centre – summary

Strengths
- Early support for parents
- Excellent early intervention for special needs
- Well-qualified staff and clear leadership
- Strong local authority policy
- Local networking and outreach
- Support/education for parents as educators of children
- Good links with health
- Close links with primary school

But
- Limited and very structured services
- No services for children without parents/carers present
- Very limited opportunities for parents as adults

Table 9.1   The Sandal Agbrigg Pre-five Centre

Services to children	Services to parents	Services to community	Links with other professionals	Funding and management
Forty-place nursery. Most children attend part-time, extended sessions with lunch if needed.	Family support team. Parent/toddler groups.	Centre available for meetings free of charge. Used by childminders (monthly).	Health (named health visitor acts as liaison with all health services).	Main funding £230,000, split between Education and Social Services.
Holiday schemes for 0 to 8-year-olds.	Adult education and interest groups.	Families in Portage scheme (monthly).	Social workers on staff. Parenting assessments for local social work teams. Training for prospective adopters.	Donations from local trusts and charities.
Medical screening for all children.	Workshops on early maths, literacy, science etc.	Asian women's craft group (weekly).		Some income from marketing home-made materials and leading training sessions, conferences etc.
Speech therapy.	'Respite' sessions where parents under stress can leave young children.	Asian Citizen's Advice Bureau (weekly).	Premises available for training use free of charge.	
Screening and support for visual and hearing impairment.	Occasional 'breathing space' sessions where nursery parents can leave younger children.			Policy and management group, with representatives from local authority.
Planned transition to primary school.	Parents' room.			Advisory liaison group, with community representatives and parents.
Full integration for children with disability, autism etc.				

9. The Sandal Agbrigg Pre-five Centre, Wakefield

Introduction

Most multi-agency centres are strategically placed in the middle of areas of considerable deprivation. Sandal Agbrigg Pre-five centre in Wakefield is an exception. It straddles very different areas. One has many large, comfortable detached homes favoured by professionals such as doctors and lawyers. The rest of the catchment area includes an estate where some families suffer intense stress and deprivation from unemployment and poverty, and an area of cramped workers' terraced cottages.

The centre opened in 1991, offering fairly standard 'combined' services. It had purpose-designed premises, with good community rooms and rooms for working with parents. A large, 40-place 'education' nursery provided part-time sessions for three to five-year-olds living in the catchment area. At the other end of the building ('*that* end', some nursery parents used to say dismissively) a 'social services' day nursery provided care for younger children, and some support for families in serious difficulties. All families could benefit from the all-day care in cases of short-term crisis.

The decision to set up a multi-agency centre was taken in 1987. Councillors and education officers, and the centre's newly appointed head, visited other combined nurseries and family centres, and were able to pick up on their successful aspects. For example, the centre closes every Wednesday afternoon to give staff time for planning, record-keeping, discussion and training: an idea that came from the Pen Green centre in Corby (see Chapter 11), and contributes a great deal to staff development. Two years after the Sandal Agbrigg centre opened, a new social worker, Kathy Stevens, was appointed. She soon came to believe that the day care centre was a fine haven for children, but did not do much for their parents. The children went home to the difficulties that had brought them into the day nursery in the first place. 'We had to try help parents do what we were doing for the children', she says.

Nursery staff, tied up with looking after children under three, had little time to help parents develop their own skills and confidence, and so

---

> ## Box 9.1   Aims of the Sandal Agbrigg Pre-five Centre
>
> Aims
> - To provide a joint service of education and care that is flexible, challenging, creative and of high quality. To enable personal growth, the enjoyment that comes with friendship, time to be active and time to reflect, to listen and be listened to.
> - To start to accept cultural diversity, to challenge gender and class stereotyping.
> - To meet the needs of individual children and families.
> - To redress various forms of deprivation experienced by children and families.
>
> Methods
> - Welcoming environment that makes positive statements to all users.
> - Provision for individual needs.
> - Multi-agency cooperation to provide a range of support and facilities. Active involvement of other agencies to reduce the incidence of abuse.
> - Quality nursery education to children living in the catchment area.
> - A challenging curriculum, broad, balanced, relevant and differentiated, providing for the spiritual, moral, cultural, mental and physical development of all children.
> - Integration of children with special needs.
> - Opportunities and activities for parents and carers to develop their knowledge, skills and understanding.
> - Training programmes for parents and carers.
> - Outreach work in the local community.
> - Assessment facilities for observation of young children.

do much more to promote the longer-term happiness and life-chances of the children. Stevens persuaded the senior staff to phase out the day nursery. Two of the nursery nurses retrained to join a new 'family support' team, working with parents on lines negotiated with them to boost their parenting skills and self-esteem. See Box 9.1

Leadership

Any description of Sandal Agbrigg Pre-five Centre in 1996 must start with Janette Smith, the head of the centre who took Wakefield's well-researched vision for a multi-agency centre and turned it into impressive reality. The daughter and grand-daughter of Yorkshire coal miners, she trained as a nursery teacher and started work in the East End of London. Soon afterwards she was put in charge of a new nursery unit attached to a school.

She had, for the time, unusually strong views on the importance of partnership with parents, and the unit rapidly became a showcase for parent involvement, much visited by York University professors and people running high-profile educational priority area projects. She went on to run two nursery schools. She is small and forthright and funny. She seems to be everywhere in the centre: sitting down with a child in the nursery or a toddler in the parent and toddler group, talking to a parent, or throwing out information and advice on the wing.

When a mother rings up saying she can't bring her child to the nursery, the head leaps into her car and goes to fetch him. No Sandal Agbrigg child is going to miss a nursery session for want of a lift while she is in charge. The child is soaking wet, but is put straight into the car regardless, and chatted to all the way back to the centre. There, Kathy Stevens – now the centre's deputy head – takes him off to change his clothes.

At Sandal Agbrigg senior staff lead by example, helping parents and children in whatever practical way they can without making judgements or standing on dignity. The motto is: 'If we do things for parents, they will do things for us.' Benevolent dictatorships have their dangers, but Janette Smith believes strongly in the importance of the professional development of the centre's staff, and has built up a team of dynamic, competent, professionals who can clearly stand up to her when necessary. At the time of my visit in 1996, she was due to retire later in the year. It was hard to imagine the centre without her driving presence and buccaneering spirit. But she will leave a staff that seems well able to carry on the high-quality work she has promoted, together with her open and accepting attitude to parents.

Family support

Kathy Stevens, the centre's senior social worker and deputy head, runs the family support service. A second qualified social worker takes part in the family support work as well as carrying other responsibilities in the centre, and there are two family workers with nursery nurse training. There are clear criteria for admission to the family support programme (see Box 9.2). A panel consisting of the head of the social work team, a local health visitor, the local infant school head, and the centre's head and deputy selects the families who are offered support, and also decides who will have the 50 per cent of nursery places that are allocated for special needs and circumstances.

When the centre changed its 'social services' work from day care to parent support, it was a daunting prospect for the nursery nurses. However, with training, a great deal of guidance and backup from the senior social worker, and a light case load to start with, they seem to have adapted well to the new demands. The two family workers in the team

---

Box 9.2   Criteria for admission to the Sandal Agbrigg family support service

- Serious difficulties in parenting that result in inclusion on the Child Protection Register or where family breakdown is a strong possibility.
- Developmental delay, seen to be the result of parenting difficulties.
- Where Parenting Assessment is required.
- Where a child has a special need, not associated with parenting difficulties.
- Where early intervention is seen as necessary to prevent future difficulties (as when there are concerns about older siblings).

---

each now handle about seven cases at any time. The work still isn't easy, and can be disheartening. But they fizz with enthusiasm, and they point to many cases where intervention has resulted in quite dramatic changes (as do less involved local health visitors and social workers). With encouragement and guidance parents, often very young and uncertain and demoralised, have gained real confidence in their own abilities. Some have gone on to further education.

The local social services team were highly sceptical about the change from day nursery to family support. However in practice the field social workers have found that the new service works well. Local day carers have filled the gap for families needing full day care. As well as referrals from health and social services, and from local schools and the centre's own nursery, parents sometimes refer themselves to the family support team. All work starts with an 'agreement meeting' (usually within a few days of referral) where parents and family workers negotiate the focus they will address. Often, parents want to talk about children's behaviour, or temper tantrums, and this becomes the starting-point.

But every case can be different: a young teenage mother might need help with budgeting and running the home: two parents who had both had special educational needs turned out to want basic sex education. The staff also act as a gateway and, when necessary, advocate to other support services, introducing parents to debt counsellors or the Citizen's Advice Bureau, or mediating with Social Security on their behalf.

Most family support sessions take place at the centre. The kitchen is a good place to get started with timid or hostile parents: making cups of tea and letting children pull out saucepans breaks the ice better than intense face-to-face discussion. If parents refuse to come in to the centre, the workers will go out to them (after checking with health visitors and others about the workers' safety). As the family support team have become more experienced, they have increasingly taken on assessments for other agencies and for court cases. Several referrals now come from outside the catchment area.

The centre offers some parents a weekly 'respite' session when staff look after their children for three hours, giving the adults time for themselves. They then discuss children's behaviour during the sessions with parents: videos of the children working and playing with staff are particularly useful for feedback. Similar – though less focused – 'breathing space' sessions are available for all nursery parents in rotation. For four weeks they can leave their babies and toddlers at the centre for three hours. These sessions started because parents asked for them – but they have the added advantage of minimising visible differences in services for 'mainstream' and 'supported' families.

All three to five-year-olds, including those in supported families, go to the centre's nursery. If families are under particular stress, or children have special needs, they are offered an extended day, with lunch. There is a special weekly session for a few children with particular needs: the staff often take them out to do everyday things like feeding the ducks in the park. Extended days are also offered to any nursery family with a short-term crisis: a mother in hospital, or a home where the electricity has been cut off in winter. (In the second case, the staff also did the family washing, and negotiated to get the electricity re-connected.)

The family support service continues during the school holidays. The centre runs three play schemes for family-supported children: a group for under-two-year-olds, one for three to fives, and one for five to nines. The regular parent and toddler groups, which are open to all parents, also continue through the holidays, as do drop-in sessions open to all nursery parents. Again, besides providing a useful service, the 'open' holiday groups help to avoid a sense of stigma for the 'supported' families.

The nursery

The 40-place nursery has superb premises: a big central space, with several rooms opening off it that are used for different activities and types of play; good outdoor play space; and an adjoining parents' room with some cooking facilities. Half the children in the nursery come in from the catchment area in the usual way. This means that the nursery's intake is genuinely comprehensive, with well-supported children from well-functioning families. This has important consequences. Staff who have worked mainly in social services establishments say it has been a revelation to discover what bright three-year-olds who get a lot of positive adult attention at home can achieve. The most articulate and self-confident children also provide models for their peers.

The other half of the intake is made up of children with special needs, either because of their own or their families' difficulties. These children are very carefully monitored and looked after. Some come with special needs assistants, who are well integrated into the work of the centre. The nursery team of four 'family workers' (NNEB or BTEC trained) is led by a qualified early years teacher. Most children come part time, for either morning or afternoon sessions.

Curriculum and assessment

When I was there in 1996 the nursery staff were beginning to re-think the layout and some of the recording and assessment arrangements (undeterred by the fact that one nursery teacher had left for promotion and the new one had not yet arrived). However, there was already meticulous attention to curriculum planning, and to assessing the progress and development of individual children. Children have plenty of choices: for example they choose when they drink their milk, and whether they go to story sessions. But staff keep a daily register of which children come to the story, so they can try to persuade non-attenders to go, or read to them individually.

The nursery was arranged with special areas for books and language, music, art, design, early writing, home play, table top toys, small world toys, the local environment, and so on. The staff were thinking of changing the areas to highlight more explicitly the different 'areas of experience' identified in the Rumbold Report (DES 1990): creative and aesthetic, mathematical, scientific, and so on. One reason was to give more visible prominence to maths and science, and to make sure that more of the nursery's excellent equipment was on open access to children every session.

There are clear curriculum policies for all the main areas, including maths, science, language and literacy, design and music. The strong policy of providing a curriculum that values all cultures is visible in displays and in the range of toys and resources for children. Two years ago the nursery's catchment area was changed, excluding and area with many Asian families. Since then the staff have been even more determined to give prominence to different cultures.

The staff monitor the quality of the work through very careful observation and record keeping. Each family worker is the 'key worker' for seven or eight children, keeping records of their activities and achievements, and building relationships with their parents or carers. At the end of every day, the nursery staff meet with the head and deputy head to discuss what all the children with identified needs did that day, together with others they have singled out for observation that week. The discussion is based on brief notes, kept through the day, and covers health, eating, and relations with carers as well as general development. Staff contact other professionals if necessary, for example alerting a health visitor about an ear infection, if a mother seems unlikely to get the child to a doctor.

Staff use a variety of records and observation methods to track the progress and plan individual programmes for all the nursery children. They undertake focused observations of how individual children go about complex activities, use tick sheets to record progress on concepts like colour or number, and keep diaries. They review the progress of every child in the nursery twice a term. There are centre-wide policies for things like display, healthy eating and bullying. The bullying policy seemed a good example of how the centre develops and implements all its policies. The local secondary school had arranged a meeting on bullying for the whole 'pyramid' of local schools. The centre's staff had taken what that offered, then arranged their own in-service session with a consultant. They then brainstormed their own policy, designed to 'empower the victim and confront the perpetrator.'

Their policy stresses preventive work: for example helping a child who finds it difficult to articulate his wishes by asking 'would you like a turn on the bike?' One of the nursery staff told me the policy was now 'well-embedded and a matter of practice. We observe children's social relationships much more closely'. This pattern of development: get in a specialist for in-service training, brainstorm, and implement seems very successful. It makes a big difference that staff have every Wednesday afternoon free for planning, discussion, and development.

The staff briefly review all policies every year, to see which are particularly successful and which need attention. As a result, talking to the staff, there seemed a high level of understanding of the policies and they did indeed seem 'well embedded'. Because the nursery is large, there are also resources for outings, and importing people to provide further enrichment for the children: artists and storytellers come in to work with them, and the resulting work by children sometimes forms the basis of a well-publicised exhibition at a local gallery.

Parent involvement in curriculum

The centre has run several curriculum workshops for parents. For example there was a set of four science workshops, focusing on science in the kitchen, in the bathroom, using toys, and 'science and myself'. Parents and staff produced an excellent booklet, with spider diagrams of science that could come out of the four areas. The bathroom diagram included steam, condensation, pressure, absorption, waves, temperature, and much more, as a basis for early scientific understanding. The work wasn't just good for parents; it also deepened the nursery workers' understanding of how everyday play can lead to science.

The centre also runs a family literacy course, with four sessions, based on materials from the Basic Skills Unit. Parents responded enthusiastically, coming in with the books they had made with their young children.

Other services for parents

There are also two weekly parent and toddler sessions, one in the morning and one in the afternoon, run by the centre's second social worker (who also happens to be NNEB qualified). The centre provides an ideal space: a big room with comfortable chairs for adults one end and tables for activities for older toddlers the other. Excellent (and, as two parents commented with approval, squeaky clean) toys are laid out for the babies and children, and adults can slip away a few at a time to make coffee in the centre's kitchen.

The centre runs various other activities for parents. Some relate to children, others are purely for interest or fun. For example there have been sessions on make-up and aromatherapy. Two years ago, Wakefield opened an adult education centre in a disused school on the edge of the nearby housing estate, with accessible and often free courses. Since then the centre has encouraged parents to go to courses there – several have done courses in computing – or introduced parents to helping in school.

My impression was that at the time of my visit, perhaps because the new member of staff responsible was finding her feet, there was not much parent demand for interest groups. But the possibility is always there: I heard two mothers chatting in the parents' room planning to ask that the centre should lay on a first aid course.

Links with other professionals

The centre has excellent links with other services, and many professionals use the centre as a base for work with local families. Every child in the nursery gets a routine medical screening. The centre also has an informal arrangement whereby the health visitor for a local GP practice acts as liaison for all health concerns, contacting the appropriate professional if there are problems. She also sits on the admissions panel and the centre's liaison group, and so takes an active part in the work of the centre.

Not all local social workers regularly use the centre, but some do, teaming up with the family support workers for assessments, and using the open and welcoming facilities, which can reassure some difficult clients, for interviews and assessments. The centre also has good links to the special education services. The local educational psychologist is often around, observing children or advising staff on individual programmes where children have problems. The local speech therapist is a regular visitor, devising programmes for children which nursery workers can then put into practice every day. Specialist teachers for hearing and visually impaired children do the same. There is good communication with the head of the local infant school, Sue Taylor, who said: 'It's very helpful to be able to get a social worker's advice when the formal involvement of social services would not be right: Kathy Stevens will come over'.

It seems likely that on any day in the centre, a visitor would see the benefits of such easy cooperation between professionals. When I was there, two autistic children had recently arrived, and the staff wanted to find out more about autism. A specialist on autism was coming in to run an in-service session the next week, and two health visitors and the Pre-school Learning Alliance coordinator both dropped by to beg places on the course. I also heard the local educational psychologist and Janette Smith decide to try to promote a support group for parents and carers with autistic children. They pooled their knowledge of local families who might be interested, and identified one child's grandmother who might act as coordinator for a new group.

The centre provides placements for several students on education and social services training courses. All students experience the whole range of the centre's work, with the appropriate special focus for education or social work. They have a professional supervisor, and a member of staff also has the job of being 'pastoral' supervisor for all the students at the centre.

Community use

Local childminders meet at the centre once a month, bringing in the pre-school children in their care. There is also a meeting once a month for parents and carers and disabled children on the Portage programme. Every Wednesday afternoon, an Asian women's craft group, and a Citizen's Advice Bureau for Asians use the centre.

All these groups organise their own creches and programmes, but the centre is a hospitable place for them, and their presence helps to widen further the experience of the centre staff. Any local group can book the centre for a meeting or training session: there is no charge for the use of the premises. Other professionals sometimes use the centre for training sessions.

Staffing and staff development

There are 13 members of staff, including the caretaker and meals supervisor. (The centre uses the school meals service in term time and Meals on Wheels in the holidays.) Two, the head and the head of the nursery, are teachers, and there are two social workers, the deputy head and one other. The six family workers all have NNEB or BTEC training. Four work mainly in the nursery and two on the parent support programme. In practice there is a lot of interchange: both groups help with the extended day and special sessions, and family-supported parents often have children in the nursery. In 1996 they were paid on scales which range from £10,500 a year to £14,500 a year. As it happens, in 1996 the second social worker and the centre's administrator both also had NNEB training, which increases the flexibility of staff even more.

Before the centre opened its planners visited other combined centres. One message that came over loud and clear was that different terms and conditions between 'social services' and 'education' staff caused considerable upsets and tensions. However, Wakefield officers saw no alternative to employing the centre's teachers – originally three, including the head, and now two – on teachers' pay and conditions, while all the nursery staff worked on local government terms and conditions, with between 20 and 26 days holiday plus 13 statutory and extra-statutory days.

At Sandal Agbrigg, differing pay and conditions have not been a significant problem. One trade-off for the less favourable local government conditions is a huge range of opportunities for in-service training. On interview, Janette Smith says she tells prospective staff: 'You will be valued for what you do, and you will get a portfolio of training that gets you where you want to go.' Another is that the work is much more varied and interesting than in many conventional institutions. 'The different pay and conditions of staff in combined centres is something that must be sorted out nationally' said Steve Chew, the education officer responsible for the centre. Janette Smith's successor will be employed on teachers' pay but local government conditions of service.

It is crucial to training and staff development that the centre is closed to children and families every Wednesday afternoon. Along with the normal five training days, it provides reasonable time for good communication, planning and reporting, and bringing outside experts in to work with. For example, a barrister has come in to prepare staff for court appearances – getting more frequent as the centre's reputation for good assessment of children and families has spread.

Increasingly, the staff themselves lead training sessions for other professionals. For example, workers have run sessions for prospective adopters, and during my visit, a request came in for staff to help train bilingual assistants in schools. Staff also get the chance to go on individual courses, and the centre contributes to the costs of those who want to study for further qualifications.

Management and funding

The total budget for Sandal Agbrigg in 1996-97 was £230,000, split between Wakefield's Social Services and Education Departments. Janette Smith and Kathy Stevens have been adept at tapping other pockets of public money, such as the GEST budget, and local trusts. For instance, the Round Table has provided a video camera, and St Catherine's, a supportive local church loans its minibus for outings and gives the centre unlimited access to its food bank and clothes store.

There is a joint Policy and Management group, including officers from the Education and Social Services departments and the head and deputy head of the centre. Within the policies set by this group, the senior staff are able to manage the centre flexibly, without detailed day to day scrutiny. This arrangement seems to work well, providing accountability without oppressive paperwork and bureaucracy.

The centre has an advisory 'liaison group'. It consists of two councillors, two local authority officers, one from education and one from social services, the local infant school head, the local health visitor, and four user representatives, two from the morning nursery and two from the afternoon. One of the user representatives, a grandfather, chairs the group. The group meets once a term. The head prepares a report, covering buildings, staffing and in-service training as well as current activities. The head sometimes refers to the group as 'governors', but they have no executive powers.

Outcomes

The centre keeps its work under constant review, and uses its Wednesday afternoons and in-service days intensively and to the full. But – not for want of asking – there has been no longitudinal study to prove that all the preventive work is effective in forestalling expensive future problems. Pat Mitchell, the head of the local social services team, has reported to her superiors that the centre's work has cut down numbers on the child protection register. She believes that early referral of parents to the centre has often forestalled the need for expensive statutory procedures.

Sue Taylor, the head of the nearby Castle Grove infants school, also believes the work of the centre is very effective. 'In a very mixed area, the nursery gives children more of an equal start: the differences are not as marked as they would otherwise be' she says, Last year the school came out as one of the best on a 'value added' analysis of Key Stage One test results for English. The Sandal Agbrigg nursery, which sends 40 or 50 children each year to the school, may well have been one of the factors responsible for this success.

Health visitors are also enthusiastic about the work of the centre. 'The progress of some parents is fantastic: recently a mother who went to special school herself has become much more assertive, and better at managing her child. It's made a real difference. Now she's pregnant again, and her confidence will affect the new baby,' said one. Another said: 'The centre has made an incredible difference, with its family support and bringing services together. A lot of preventive work is done here. Without it there would just be me, and my caseload of 300 families.'

Janette Smith says: 'I had a vision.' The vision was of a centre where professionals worked together to give parents practical, non-judgmental support, and to give children the opportunities needed for their full social, emotional and intellectual development. Helped by a supportive local authority, prepared to give her her head, she seems to have more than succeeded. Her staff – the vast majority of them nursery nurses – are so enthusiastic and self-starting that newcomers can find them daunting. The use made of the centre by other professionals, for assessment and a base for their work, seems to be growing as its reputation spreads.

To a visitor, the quality and attention to detail are remarkable. The centre is full of fresh flowers and fruit. The nursery is spotless, meticulously set out at the beginning of every session, as is the room for parent and toddler sessions. Relations with parents are visibly warm and open. Children with special needs or disabilities are unobtrusively integrated, and their progress is kept under close scrutiny. There is individual attention to children whose development is unusually advanced, as well as those whose development is delayed.

Janette Smith's biggest regret is that Social Services as a whole, while supportive and appreciative of the work the centre does, have not become more involved, possibly because Education was given the lead administrative responsibility at County Hall level, and because of other pressures on the local Social Services team. She also regrets that Wakefield has not followed up by opening another combined centre. Wakefield has two other Social Services family centres, which have been reorganised to provide family support rather than day care. But they are only for 'referred families': Social Services has said that they only have resources for 'stigmatised provision'.

On the education side Steve Chew, the line manager for the centre, says that 'Sandal Agbrigg is a very successful centre, and a model for us'. But, he says, when both education and social services budgets have had to find successive cuts, it is just too expensive to replicate. 'The cost of places at Sandal Agbrigg would get us two and a half times as many places in nursery classes'. And that, in a nutshell, is one of the problems of good multi-agency nursery centres. However great their long-term benefits to children and parents, and however successful they are in preventing later deep-rooted and expensive educational and social problems, their costs are always likely to look high when measured against conventional provision over the short term.

Box 9.3 Sandal Agbrigg – summary

Strengths
- Dynamic leadership.
- Strong social work and education inputs from staff.
- Family support and preventive work.
- Good delivery of health services.
- High-quality nursery taking children from wide range of backgrounds.
- Good integration for special needs.
- Curriculum and literacy workshops for parents.
- Building well-used by others working with children.

But
- No mainstream day care.
- Few activities on premises for parents to develop new interests.
- Seen as expensive and difficult to replicate.

Table 10.1   The ACE Centre, Chipping Norton

Services for parents and children	Services for adults	Links with outside professionals	Funding and management
Drop-in family centre for parents and children.	Variety of adult classes.	Family centre managed by local social work team.	Funding from Oxfordshire for nursery school and family centre: other services from three year grants from the Rural Development Commission.
Creche for adults at classes or shopping.	Training for professionals and voluntary groups.	Family centre staff take part in assessments.	
Nursery school with part-time places.	Computer centre, open to local community and local businesses. Courses at all levels from basic literacy and	Community education runs classes at centre.	Computer centre set to cover own costs when RDC grant runs out.
After school care for five to 12-year-olds.	computing upwards.		
Holiday play scheme for five to 12-year-olds.	Computer training on- and off-site.		Education department manages school and community education: social services manages family centre.
Toy library.			Other services managed by a local Trust set up for the purpose in 1996.

10. The ACE Centre, Chipping Norton

Introduction

Chipping Norton is a small rural market town in West Oxfordshire. It has one main employer, Parker Knoll, and it is surrounded by farming communities with pockets of considerable poverty and isolation. It is an attractive town in lovely countryside, but it has always been very different from its smart and famous Cotswold neighbours such as Stow on the Wold and Moreton in Marsh. It is said to be an insular place, where people in trouble button their lip and put up with considerable difficulties, rather than looking for services and support.

In the late 1980s various professionals in the area were becoming well aware of local families' increasing problems. For example, one of the town's primary heads noticed that many mothers, who were ostensibly coming in to talk about their children, ended up by talking about themselves, their struggles, loneliness and depression. She also noticed that many children were coming into school at five without the basic social and learning skills she had come to expect at their age. To explore these issues, the area education officer organised a meeting for a range of professionals, from health, social services and community education.

Then two local primary schools were merged, leaving empty most of an infants school building in the centre of town. The only occupant was a 40-place nursery school. The ACE Centre (ACE stands for Activities, Child care and Education) had become possible, and it opened in 1994. Alongside the nursery school, the centre now offers a new drop-in family centre, run by social services; a computer centre; a creche; after school and holiday play schemes; various community education classes for adults and under-fives; premises available at reasonable rates for local groups; and a base for outreach support for parents and other people working with under fives in the local area.

The Oxfordshire context

In 1985, there was a change of political control in Oxfordshire. A new hung council took over from the Conservatives. The next year it set up an early years working party. Given the low level of pre-school provision in the county, councillors wanted to develop partnerships with the voluntary and private sectors, in order to extend provision. (In 1996 the working party developed into a fully fledged early years joint subcommittee of the education and social services committees.) Local panels were set up in Oxfordshire's divisions, bringing together a wide range of people from education, health, social services and the voluntary sector to look at needs in their area.

The council also appointed an officer in the economic development office whose job was to try to promote more child care services. The link between child care, training and jobs for women was explicit from the start. The first idea was to build partnerships with the private sector. There were some initial successes, with nurseries set up in partnership with other agencies, and some large companies establishing their own nurseries. But smaller companies were not interested, and there was a need for more community-based provision. So the search was on for any combination of available building and external funding that could improve services for under-fives and their parents in areas where families most needed them.

A Training and Enterprise Council scheme provided money to set up after school and holiday play schemes. One such scheme started in Chipping Norton at the school which was to become the ACE Centre. The Rural Development Commission (RDC), gave a small grant to help get it off the ground. Outreach work in the area had also started, with the appointment of an early years development worker who helped to start playgroups in villages, and provide flexible training for people working with young children in any setting – parents, childminders, voluntary groups and private ventures.

So there was a receptive policy structure in place when local professionals suggested that the vacated school building in Chipping Norton might be used for a multi-agency centre for under fives and their families, providing support, child care, community education and training, and a base for the outreach work. The missing ingredient was extra funding. Happily the Rural Development Commission had identified the North Cotswolds as a suitable area for its Countryside Employment scheme, and was looking to set up demonstration projects. It was prepared to come in as a major partner in the bigger project.

The RDC put up £109,000 over three years for core revenue costs and some capital funding. Oxfordshire agreed to refurbish the building, and to set up an open access family centre run by social services. The ACE Centre was under way. The RDC later gave a separate grant to help launch a new computer centre on the site. The ACE Centre has a part-time coordinator, paid through the RDC grant, who is responsible for the community parts of the building, the creche, and the holiday and after school schemes. The nursery school, family centre and computer centre stayed as separate entities within the project, each with its own head and line of management.

Box 10.1   Aims of the ACE Centre

Mission
To endeavour to be a focal point within the local area for the provision of family support, childcare and community development.

Aims
- To address the issues of family needs, particularly for those who are geographically or socially isolated.
- To provide local child care and support local child care providers.
- To provide community education, recreation and vocational training activities.
- To provide a base for community groups and self-help schemes.

Note: ACE stands for Activities, Childcare and Education.

The family centre

The family centre is open to all comers between 9am and 3pm every day. So far there has been no limit on numbers, though at times 60 people use it, and spill out to the small outdoor play area. The use of the centre built up fast, and the staffing went up from two to two and a half. However recent cuts in the social services budget meant that they were about to go back to two again. The family workers I talked to both had experience of 'closed door' family centres, dealing only with families who had been referred, and much preferred the open centre. 'There's much less stigma here, and it's much friendlier', said one. 'I've learnt a lot more about family life, and how people manage in spite of real difficulties.' The other said: 'We have a blank sheet – we can meet people's needs'.

The family centre is housed in the old nursery school building (the nursery moved into space vacated by the primary school, with Oxfordshire meeting the refurbishment costs). It has a big double room, an outdoor play area, a small kitchen where parents can make themselves drinks and snacks, and a separate office that can also be used for private interviews. It's a nice informal space, comfortable for adults and interesting for children. The main ACE Centre creche is in a room off the open space. It's a good arrangement: mothers dropping their children at the creche become more aware of the family centre's existence, and at quiet times the children in the creche and their workers can come out into the bigger area. A mother with a demanding toddler can drop him or her in the creche, and be able to concentrate on her younger child in the family centre.

Because the family centre is genuinely open to all, a good cross-section of local people has started to use it freely. Parents who have been referred by a social worker or health visitor mix in easily: there is no stigma attached to the referral. The workers go out to clients' homes when more private and sensitive work is needed. They work on parenting skills, supervise children coming back home from care, and take part in court assessments. 'We try to be clear and specific about what we're doing. If families seem stuck, we do short pieces of work, and then evaluate – we could spend for ever and a day with some families otherwise.'

The family workers link with other relevant professionals – social workers, clinical psychiatrists, solicitors, health visitors – in this work. As well as working with parents, they also take on some one-to-one work with children. They have run a successful 'nurturing group' where parents and children, meeting both separately and together, discussed parenting issues such as setting boundaries and rules, negotiation and praise. They hope to repeat it, provided they can find leaders capable of running the children's group, where deep emotional issues can surface unexpectedly.

In the first 18 months, the family centre has had several successes. 'The ACE location is very important. It encourages parents to look beyond to the other recreational and educational opportunities' said one of the workers. For example, a mother who used to be bussed miles away to a family centre in Banbury was unable to leave her house by herself when she was first brought to the ACE Centre. After a time at the new local family centre, she began to bring her children on her own. Then she moved on to do a basic education course, involving work on computers. 'People can filter through to something they feel they can tackle', said a family worker.

The family centre has proved a good informal place for other activities. An English course for speakers of other languages runs there: it seems a more comfortable and inviting location that the centre's classroom. There have been basic education classes, and a multi-cultural 'return to learn' group. There was a successful Saturday morning drop-in for fathers. Health visitors have come in for informal discussions and have run a post-natal group, a bereavement group, and a healthy eating group. The benefits agency also came in twice a week to offer advice, but the service had to end when funding was cut,

There is a permanent toy library whenever the centre is open – any parent can pay £2 a year, and then borrow any toy at the centre (within reason) for a charge of 25p for two weeks. The staff are managed by the local social services team manager, Jo Powell. She is convinced of the benefits of a small local and open centre: 'You can be more innovative about what you do: you're not tied down. You don't have to do quite so much writing and record-keeping, which can form a barrier right away.'

The creche

The creche is in many ways the linchpin of the ACE Centre's separately managed component parts. It is a vital ingredient in the success of the adult and community education and the computer centre. It's a flexible affair. The main creche can take up to eight children, but if more space is needed, a second creche for up to 11 children over two can be run in the 'family room', which is also used as a base for the after school scheme. Parents pay £1.80 an hour. There are two permanent part-time staff, with sessional workers when more are needed. School students on child care courses regularly help out.

People attending daytime classes at the centre are regular users. But the ACE Centre's convenient location in the middle of town means the creche is also ideal for parents who just want to do their shopping in peace. The creche (or creches) burst at the seams for some classes, such as keep fit. In the holidays, the creche runs for seven hours a week.

The play scheme and out-of-school club

Both these schemes started before the ACE Centre opened, and were based in the primary school. The ACE Centre coordinator is now in over-all charge of them, and they are run by a leader who is paid to work a 24 hour week. The holiday play scheme can take up to 32 five to twelve-year-olds. It costs £1.80 an hour (with discounts for siblings), and offers flexible hours to meet parents' needs. It runs every half term and holiday, from 8.30am to 6.00pm. Social services have the option to book up to 25 per cent of the places, through they haven't yet taken their full allocation.

There were some teething problems, not least in organising a system where parents pay in advance and have to give 48 hours notice of a cancellation. In a mixed neighbourhood, there was also, at first, a tendency for richer parents, some with their own nannies, to book out the service. A clear admissions policy, with priorities for single and working parents, helped to sort that out. As the scheme has developed, so has the range of activities offered, with more structured opportunities for sports, drama and music led by qualified people.

Staff have developed equal opportunities policies, and a simple behaviour management policy that includes a commitment to talk problems over with parents, and the right to send children home. 'It's a wonderful scheme, and people come from a long way away for it', said a parent. The play scheme has benefited from the range of facilities in the ACE

Centre. As well as using the old school hall, younger children are sometimes taken over to the family centre and creche for a quiet time.

The out of school club takes up to 20 children, who are collected each day from three local primary schools. It is only registered for five to 12-year-olds, which means the centre cannot offer extended day facilities for nursery parents. Children can settle down to a variety of activities – printing, sticking, reading, playing with My Little Pony, playing mini-snooker. The cost is £5.50 a session, including a cooked tea.

Both schemes work to a very tight budget. As a directly managed part of the ACE Centre, money for staff training and development had to come out of a budget that was already very tight indeed. In future, both schemes may be expected to cover more of their costs, but the management is determined not to compromise the service they offer to poorer families.

The computer centre

The computer centre was also launched with financial help from the Rural Development Commission, which gave £16,000 for equipment, provided matching funds could be raised. Contributions from the District Council (£5000), British Telecom (£5000), Apple computers (£5000 worth of equipment), and local fund-raising provided the other half of the capital costs. The RDC has also paid the full manager's salary in the first year, and a diminishing proportion over the following two years. The intention is that the computer centre should completely cover its costs when the grant runs out at the beginning of 1998, and it seems well on target to do so.

The computer centre is on the side of the ACE building, accessible from the main centre, but also with its own entrance. 'At first I thought the computer centre was here simply because there was some space in the building', said Debra Barnes, the part-time manager, who came from industry to set up the centre. 'Now I see the point. The nursery and creche and play schemes mean women can come to classes, and the computers can be used by community groups'.

There are courses ranging from absolute beginners through to complex applications. Basic education and literacy classes also use the facilities, so computer literacy can be gained alongside basic English. Some of the classes help to produce brochures and posters for community groups, and for the ACE Centre itself. The local community education council is responsible for the computer centre. Many of the courses are charged at the normal adult education rates, with concessions for people who are unemployed and on low-incomes. Classes run on Saturdays as well as weekdays, and through the holidays (apart from August, when there is little demand).

Wednesdays are reserved for local businesses, and several have begun to use the centre for training. They are charged commercial, but competitive rates. Individuals can come in and use the machines, or the Internet link, for £5 an hour. The centre also arranges consultants to go out to people's homes and offices to train on the spot, at a charge of £25 an hour.

The computer centre's use as a local resource for schools is growing. As well as plans to bring the nursery school children in from time to time, six week 'twilight' courses for sixth formers started in 1996, with the local secondary school meeting half the costs. Altogether, the computer centre was described a 'runaway success'. It is an unusual resource for a rural area, and very well used. In its first 15 months, it provided courses for over 300 people, 55 of them women seeking to return to the labour market. Two hundred people signed up for NVQ and other vocational qualifications.

Other adult and community education

'There are always a significant number of community education clients who won't set foot in a school, even when the facilities are excellent' said Mike Bardsley, the community education coordinator for Chipping Norton, and one of the original local promoters of the ACE Centre. The centre is an ideal base for them, less formal than the secondary school and available in the daytime, with a creche and the nursery school for children. Community education has run various courses there, such as keep fit, return to learn, pottery, gym and activity classes for under-fives, family literacy: 'significant work we couldn't have done elsewhere' says Mike Bardsley.

It has proved more expensive to run courses at ACE than originally expected, but the difference has been averaged out across the whole community education programme. In some cases, such as the family literacy course, it was a shortage of funds for tutors rather than shortage of customers that limited the service.

Several people said they would like the adult education on offer to be more informal, and more responsive to requests from users, supplementing the slightly ad hoc menu currently on offer, But management and financial constraints (see *Management and funding,* below) have made it difficult to consult potential clients and develop the services they want. People in the community who want to run classes can also rent the centre. The ACE coordinator manages the lets. Various classes, such as Tai Chi and keep fit, have been run privately.

The nursery school

The nursery school has 40 places. Almost all the children are four-year-olds, and all come part-time. Demand for places is so high that staff had not so far felt able to take children younger, and (to everyone's regret) no way had been found to offer any provision for lunch or extended hours. Since local schools are increasingly admitting four-year-olds at the beginning of the school year, some children only have two terms in the nursery, and there was concern that nursery vouchers would accelerate this trend.

The new developments in the ACE Centre did not yet seem to have greatly affected the nursery school – although parents have been able to benefit from the creche and new opportunities for adult education. However there had been good communication between school staff and family workers about some individual children's and families' needs, and curriculum links had started to develop between the nursery and family centre. For example, they had held a joint celebration of the Hindu festival Diwali.

The nursery head teacher, Jeanne Peskett, took over in 1996. She came from London, where she had been involved in other multi-agency projects. Like the other centre managers, she would like to develop better integration between the centre's parts. But her first priority was to make sure the school's curriculum and record-keeping responded to the new challenges from OFSTED. With the wholehearted approval of staff, record-keeping and assessment have been comprehensively re-thought. They threw out long checklists of what children could (or, as it more often seemed to workers and parents, could not) do, and introduced a learning profile based on careful observation and recording of children's achievements in different curriculum areas.

The nursery has two teachers (including the head, who gets a day a week's cover for planning and administration) and two nursery nurses. They all take responsibility for a group of 10 children each session. Every week they nominate one child from each group, and observe those children through the whole of the next week. All children are observed at least once each term: those with special needs rather more frequently. Staff say the new system of records and observation is 'much better for planning, and for extending children' than the old checklists.

The nursery school has always had a community focus, running open sessions every Friday. Every other week is Family Friday: any parent can bring children in the morning to play with the equipment, and chat to the staff. The other Fridays are taken up alternately by playgroups, and by minders and nannies. Julie Fisher, an Oxfordshire early years Inspector, says: 'It's an ideal way of spreading good practice in the community, with the nursery school at the hub.' In practice, according to the staff, the Family Fridays are 'wonderful'. There is good take-up (sometimes almost too good – 'we can hardly move'), staff can 'have a good chat with parents', discussing anything from strategies to deal with behaviour problems to ways of colouring rice for children to play with.

The staff consider that the other Open Fridays are of more variable benefit. The nannies' and minders' Fridays provide a place for lonely au pairs to network, but not always much more. Some playgroups are wonderful, and there are productive discussions and exchanges: others simply come in and use the facilities and equipment, sometimes leaving staff to sort it all out again afterwards.

Training, development and outreach

Each component part of the ACE Centre organises training for its own staff, although at the time of my visit there were some plans to run courses for all staff on practical matters such as first aid, and to open those courses to users. A small budget was set aside at the start for training the staff of the centre's new services, in particular the play scheme and creche. The early years outreach worker for West Oxfordshire, who moved her base to the new centre when it opened, has helped to find appropriate training courses, and in 1996, a training strategy for the centre was being developed with Oxfordshire County Council. The centre is used as a base for a Pre-school Learning Alliance diploma course in playgroup practice, and the nursery and the family centre both offer practice placements for students in training.

Kris Gillam, the early years outreach worker, says that the new centre has made an excellent 'child friendly' base for flexible training to meet the needs for everyone working with under eightsin the area – parents, voluntary groups, childminders, and private ventures as well as teachers and nursery workers in the statutory sector. She also has a van, equipped with toys and resources, which she takes out to village halls and community centres. Within six weeks, it is often possible to establish demand, identify possible leaders to continue the group, and arrange suitable training for them. She has organised a number of courses at the centre for workers and parents, covering topics they have asked for, such as first aid, food hygiene, work for NVQs in child care, planning for nursery vouchers, management and fund-raising.

Management and funding

The ACE Centre started with very tight funding. Oxfordshire put in a lot of invaluable support, both in resources to refurbish the building, and in officer and administrative time. But the core running costs of the coordinator, creche, and play schemes had to come out of the RDC grant, together with any revenue that the centre could raise. As a result, the coordinator was appointed to work only part-time for 25 hours a week, at £7 an hour. This had to cover administration of the centre, setting up the creche, recruiting staff for the creche and playscheme, supervising quality, and generally developing and publicising the centre.

There is general agreement that the coordinator's hours (and pay) were inadequate. There were administrative hiccoughs too. Financial administration was organised through Oxfordshire, and in a new multi-agency centre there were a lot of difficulties about miscoded accounts. Tracking and sorting out errors took up a lot of the scarce administrative time. Different funders wanted management reporting and accounts in different forms. All this detracted from the vital job of publicising the new centre, researching what services users wanted, and developing them.

The three largest component parts of the centre – the family centre, nursery school and computer centre – all ran independently, with their own lines of management supervision. The nursery head, not the coordinator, was the site manager. The three managers met regularly with the coordinator, and tried to develop a centre ethos and ways of sharing resources and equipment, but most of their time was taking up in establishing their own service, and there could be no dynamic leadership of the centre as a whole. 'We could write a handbook on how *not* to set up a combined centre', said one local professional. 'It's a great shame the project wasn't given a delegated budget and full time coordinator from the start. It limited the potential growth and development.'

The first coordinator left in the summer of 1996. A scheme was devised to create a full-time post without new core funding by combining a 25 hours as centre coordinator with 15 hours for nursery school administration. It was a curious hybrid of a job, calling for imaginative development work alongside organising the nursery children's milk, but it was still a great improvement. Administrative and accounting problems were also being sorted out. In the autumn of 1996 a specially formed local trust took over the management of the centre. The school, family centre and computer centre will continue to be run by Oxfordshire education and social services departments: the other centre functions will be managed by the Trust and coordinator.

Financial constraints may remain the block to further development. The computer centre is well on the way to covering its costs by the time its tapering Rural Development Commission grant runs out at the beginning of 1998. The costs of the other community services, such as the creche and play scheme, and the coordinator's salary – altogether a minimum of about £50,000 a year – will have to be found elsewhere when the main RDC grant comes to an end in June 1997. This may lead to a conflict between making services available to the neediest families, and using the facilities to raise revenue. In 1996, the centre was likely to raise about £24,000 from fees and fund-raising.

The new Trust is hoping that fund-raising from the Lottery, Children in Need, and other sources will help to bridge the funding gap. Oxfordshire has a big investment in the centre, and there is some solid backing at senior officer level. But when the County Council is likely to have to cut millions of pounds from its budget in 1997, extra support – or even the continuation of existing services – is by no means certain.

In spite of these difficulties, the ACE centre has achieved a great deal. The demand for its services is well established. The project has successfully begun to bring different services together. The centre was designed as a national pilot project for services in rural areas, and its experience will be built on elsewhere. In its short existence the centre has offered new opportunities and support to local families, enabled several of its users to find employment, and supported a great many families. It may not yet have succeeded in being much more than the sum of its parts – but the parts have offered important new services. Local professionals say that some of the most disadvantaged members of the community have benefited. 'A number of people's lives have been changed by the ACE centre's existence. It's a firm footing to build on', concluded a member of the original local project team.

Box 10.2   The ACE Centre – summary

Strengths
- Accessible drop-in centre for rural area
- Open access family support
- Community education, including computer centre, with creche
- Building with potential to develop new services
- Base for outreach to villages
- Quality nursery education
- After school and holiday care

But
- Divided management – no overall leadership
- Uncertain funding of core services
- No all day care or flexible nursery hours
- Little education for under-fours

Table 11.1   The Pen Green Centre, Northamptonshire

Services for children	Services for parents and adults	Links with other professionals	Funding and management
Nursery education for two to four-year-olds.	Big range of open groups and classes. Some closed therapeutic groups. Many accredited courses – NVQ Open University, GCSE and A-level. Basic education.	Two social workers on the staff.	Main funding £325,000 a year split between County Education and Social Service Departments.
Two playgroups.		Excellent relations with local health visitors.	
Creche all day and some evenings.	Curriculum groups. Men's group. Training project for unemployed.	Local health professionals help to lead a variety of groups.	Other funding from Social Services, European Community, charities, some fees, and income generated by participation in conferences and courses.
After school club once a week for five to 11s. Youth club.	Weekly health clinic. Free pregnancy testing and family planning. Free legal advice.		Delegated budget overseen by policy group, with representatives from local authority and parents.
Nuture group for children in need.	Community lunches.		
Groups for younger children with parents.	Home Start scheme.		
	Scrap recycling project.		
Holiday play schemes (including semi-integrated special needs scheme) for four to 11-year-olds.	Family holidays and trips.		
Weekly open drop-in play session for parents and children.	Employment opportunities.		

11. Pen Green Centre for under fives and their families, Corby

Introduction

In the world of early years centres, Pen Green is the big one. Thousands of professionals have visited the centre, and their main response seems to be: 'If only...'. If only *everyone* could have the space, the time for staff training and development, the seemingly generous resources, the commitment and enthusiasm of so many volunteers. In fact, the Pen Green staff, users and supporters have fought hard to develop services that fulfil the original vision: a 'one-stop shop' aiming to meet the educational, social and health needs of young children, their families, and their neighbourhood.

'Nothing was easy, nothing was handed to them on a plate', said one observer. At one stage, when Conservatives took over Northamptonshire County Council in the late 1980s, parents had to campaign for the survival of everything but a basic nursery school. Their impassioned descriptions to councillors of what the centre's range of services had done for them carried the day.

When Pen Green opened in 1983, Corby was a steel town whose livelihood had just closed down. It has gradually changed, with new housing, new young families moving in, new light industry, and new jobs, many of them insecure, low-paid and part-time. But unemployment is still high, and the need for child care, support, accessible heath services, help for families of children with special needs, and adult education and training seem if anything to have increased. The centre now offers a huge range of services for children and adults, based round four interlocking strands of work: a community nursery; family support; health work; and adult and community education. Many professionals, from health visitors to lawyers, take part. But the range of activities is only half the story.

What is most exciting, and sometimes daunting, about Pen Green is the spirit in which the services are offered. The aim is that the views and feelings of local families should be paramount. To that end all professional practices are subject to continual review, research and criticism by staff and parents. The commitment is challenging as well as exhilarating.

Empowerment

Empowerment has always been at the core of Pen Green's philosophy. Northamptonshire decided to set up a multi-agency early years centre in a disused comprehensive school in Corby in 1981. There was consultation with local parents early on to find out what services they wanted in an area that had no local authority day care, few playgroups, and no organisations to support young families. The original vision for the centre came from more than one source. A local councillor had campaigned strongly for a one-stop shop where parents of young children could find the services they needed. The local social work team leader was concerned that social work should be preventive as well as crisis-oriented.

The catalyst that turned the vision into reality was Margy Whalley, a former teacher and community worker. She had worked abroad, in Brazil and Papua New Guinea. Before coming to Pen Green she had run a Home Start project, organising volunteers to support new or struggling parents. Often the best volunteers were women who had once needed support themselves. In her varied career, she had developed very strong notions of participation and empowerment for users, both children and adults, and for staff. So the message of openness and participation at Pen Green was unusually strong. From the beginning, parents have been directly involved in staff appointments and decisions about priorities and the use of the building.

Empowerment was a fashionable concept at the time among community and youth workers. But it is easier said than done. At Pen Green, they seem to have done it. Many parents at Pen Green tell you that when they came to the centre they felt worthless, depressed, and isolated. The opportunities offered by Pen Green were a lifeline.

Some have gone on to run adult groups at the centre. Others run the centre's two playgroups, or work in the creche or the holiday play scheme (Pen Green is a good generator of paid employment for local people). Many have gone on to further training and education, or found other routes to new careers and employment. Former Pen Green parents run groups and projects as volunteers, and become parent governors at local schools, and community leaders. 'It's brilliant' said a single parent who got involved in some groups, then worked in the playgroup, then started leading groups, and was now doing an NVQ Level 3 in child care. 'You get so much support here. Everyone is bubbling and welcoming.'

Most of the beneficiaries have been women. But Pen Green has also set out to include fathers as participants in the centre, starting by deliberately recruiting male staff to the original all-women team. In the late

1980s a men's group started, and several men joined the many women who have found a new sense of direction and enterprise through Pen Green. The centre has been part of a recent European Commission project on men and child care.

It would be absurd to pretend that all professional barriers between staff and users have broken down. But the constant striving for real equality and participation, and for new ways of making the centre friendly and accessible to all comers, is evident, and the results are impressive. Parents and users can contribute to, or criticise, the centre's management in various ways. There is an informal monthly Centre Forum, open to all comers, whose meetings are minuted and acted on. The centre's formal Policy Group has two elected users on it. In the nursery, there are regular meetings for parents in their family worker groups. When Pen Green staff contribute to professional conferences, parents take part in the presentation. Through all these routes, parents can and do challenge the centre's staff, and some of their decisions.

Box 11.1   Pen Green philosophy

- Inter-agency collaboration.
- Open access – not just 'problem families'.
- Locally based – bring services to parents.
- Power sharing – challenging the nature of parent-professional and child-professional relationships.
- Parents as partners, managers, and service providers.
- Complement parent expertise, discouraging dependence, encouraging empowerment.

Building and services

The centre, including the nursery, is open for 50 weeks a year, closing for the first two weeks in August. A good way to see the range of services on offer is simply to tour the buildings. From the start, Pen Green had the advantage of generous space: it could expand into new parts of the disused secondary school buildings. But the premises – daunting classrooms with high ceilings and windows – were not ideal for young children and needed a lot of work to make them friendly and accessible. The current layout and equipment is the result of a lot of experiment, and of energetic fundraising.

The main nursery building has a large open nursery, with a big outdoor play area. The nursery spills out into a wide corridor with administrative offices off it (children seem welcome to spill into the offices, too). Across the corridor from the offices is the 'Family Room', open to all comers from 8.30am to 4pm every day except for Wednesday afternoons.

The room has a kitchen at one end, and the worker in charge cooks lunch for those who want it: 'She leads from behind the coffee', as one parent put it. She makes sure that territorial cliques do not take over, and newcomers are made welcome, and organises groups and discussions.

Pen Green rapidly found it could not meet the demand for nursery places. It now has two separate playgroups, one morning and one after-noon, which share a big room opening on to a large outdoor play area, which includes a 'sonic playground' – an imaginative resource for all the children using the centre, and particularly those with special needs. These spaces are also used once a week for the after school club for prim-ary children, and for two holiday play schemes, one with 40 places for local children, and one for children with special needs.

There is a big creche, which runs all day and in the evenings when there are adult groups and classes. The creche is free (apart from a 20p contribution for snacks): the playgroups have to cover their costs, and charge £2 a session. Both are staffed by paid workers, most of them former nursery parents and users, trained at Pen Green. The staff have given a lot of attention to 'heuristic play', providing suitable materials to help babies and young children explore and learn in the creche and in the groups for parents and younger children.

The creche has its own crawl-through hatch to the centre's big soft play area, with a ball pool and a variety of soft blocks and bags for jump-ing, climbing, and thumping. There is also a Snoezelen room, a relaxing place with calming music and sophisticated lighting affects. These excel-lent resources can be used by all the children and adults on site – as well as by individual parents and children. The former school gym is used for dance and keep fit and football. There are two offices, one used for a European Social Fund training project for unemployed people, and the other by the local Home Start scheme, and by a free legal advice service once a month. There is also a youth club, and a cost-covering scrap resources project which now serves the whole of Northamptonshire.

Pen Green staff and users started most of these projects. Home Start began as a go-it-alone venture called Family Friends, and is now run by the national charity and funded by the local authority. An assistant care-taker wanted to do something constructive for the young people hanging out round the site, and started a volunteer-run youth club, which only attracted local authority funding when it was already well established.

Finally, upstairs in the second building, there are two large converted classrooms used for group work, and a small office which is useful for one-to-one sessions. One of the group rooms is set out for pre-nursery children and adults, with toys and climbing equipment and dens for the children. It is used for drop-in parent and child groups and the weekly health clinic. The other is furnished for adults on their own, and used for adult groups and training.

It is a big, busy centre, but there are many ways into it for a nervous first-time user. Once in, the free creche makes it easy to join one of the wide range of adult groups. The nursery is the entry point for many users. It's a rule that a parent of new nursery child must spend two weeks at the nursery while their child settles in. During that time, parents also learn about what the centre can provide for them as adults. 'The nursery gets you started, gets you involved' said one father.

The family room is another non-threatening way in. So are the weekly baby massage and aromatherapy sessions, which health visitors often recommend to stressed or isolated parents. The weekly health clinic is a fourth entry point, attracting parents when their children are still babies. It offers coffee, social life, and toys and space for children to play, as well as checks and advice from a health visitor. 'It's a good way for people to become a person, not just a Mum', said one regular attender.

Staff are still not satisfied that the most vulnerable people will find their way to the centre. 'People can still see it as somewhere where officials are watching you', said one of the two social workers on the staff. She was considering recruiting a team of parents, who had found the centre difficult at first, to help draw others in.

Development and training

Early on, Margy Whalley and her senior colleagues negotiated that staff should have a significant amount of time each week for staff planning and development. They believed this was essential if staff – many with only a child care training – were to develop quality work with children and adults, in an area where people suffered a great deal of economic and social stress. Every week, on Wednesday afternoon, there is a three and a half hour staff meeting, which can be used for planning, review or training sessions. The nursery family workers have a further one and a half hour meeting late on Monday afternoons. The whole staff meets to review practice for two full days every year. All staff have regular supervisions every month, and five and a half hours non-contact time every week (including the regular meetings).

Almost all the workers take part in further education or training in their spare time, with the centre contributing to the costs. Workers have taken advanced diplomas, degrees and masters degrees in child care and education, and a wide range of qualifications relevant to the centre's work, such as community education, social work, family therapy, play therapy, and counselling, and dance. Everyone who works in the centre, as a member of staff, sessional worker or volunteer has some induction training, covering things like assertiveness, group work, and child protection. Parents and others who are interested in helping to lead groups for adults are given special training. The centre's interest in research has also promoted review and development, and involved volunteers and parents as well as staff.

Staff join other adults in assertiveness groups, GCSE maths and English classes, and Open University courses. Consultants come in regularly to help with management, team-building, and curriculum development. The nursery curriculum expert runs sessions for parents as well as staff. Pen Green is now an NVQ accreditation centre, with three members of staff qualified as assessors, and several users have gained qualifications in child care at the centre. The centre has participated in international projects, bringing links with nurseries in Denmark and Italy, which widened perspectives and showed new ways of approaching nursery organisation and curriculum.

'You have to make opportunities for staff', said Margy Whalley. 'They all need to be rigorous thinkers: they are all required to study, research, observe children's development, and communicate with parents and visit their homes. But they constantly amaze me, in their quest to learn.' 'I love working here – it's so *interesting*', said one of the family workers in the nursery.

Groups

Once across the threshold, Pen Green offers its users an extensive range of groups and courses at all levels, from basic literacy to Open University preparatory courses, and from baby massage to a writers' workshop. (See Table 11.2) There are groups for parents as parents, and parents as people. Some groups work for academic and vocational qualifications. Others meet to discuss topics they have chosen in an unstructured way. The local college is a bus ride away, and has no creche. Pen Green provides a familiar and accessible stepping stone to further qualifications and study. The college values the work, and provides some tutors, a base for some specially tailored courses, and practical support, as does the local Worker's Educational Association.

There are open groups for all comers, and closed, longer term, more therapeutic groups, such as the group for survivors of sexual abuse, where members decide when and whether newcomers can take part. Parents and other professionals such as health visitors and midwives, lead the groups. Almost all the Pen Green workers run groups alongside their other full-time responsibilities. Their range of professional backgrounds, in social work, education, nurseries, community work and voluntary work, is an invaluable resource. Every ten weeks all the group leaders – professionals and volunteers – meet to review their successes and failures, and discuss new groups, resources, and any further training that might be relevant to leaders.

Table 11.2   Groups at Pen Green: Summer 1996

Monday	Tuesday	Wednesday	Thursday	Friday
Morning Special Needs (for parents and carers of children with special needs)	*Morning* Allsorts (a different subject every week) First steps (parents and children 1–2) Psychology GCSE	*Morning* Drop-in (open House in the nursery for children up to 5 and their carers) Our changing selves (Open University course) Maths GCSE	*Morning* Baby massage Prenancy testing Home Start meeting	*Morning* U2 (drop-in messy play for under 2s and their carers) Step families
Afternoon Choices (for women who have suffered sexual abuse) Craft workshop Baby massage Yoga relaxation	*Afternoon* Parents as Educators (How children learn and how to support them) Baby Clinic Young Mums Group	*Afternoon* NVQ (in child care, levels 2 and 3). Young Ones (parent-run parent and toddler group using the main nursery). Maths GCSE	*Afternoon* Communicating with teenagers Early daze (support groups for parents of 0–1-year-olds – creche for older children) Great Expectations (pregnancy support group)	*Afternoon* In Betweenies (messy play for toddlers) Single Parents support group
Evening Communicating skills Handling stress	*Evening* Writer's group (for women who like to write their feelings, thoughts and ideas down)		*Evening* After school club The Alexander Men's Group (share your thoughts and feelings about being a man)	*Evening* Youth Club

Pen Green's extensive community education programme is the only part of its work that has not received secure local authority funding, and a lot of the work depends on the goodwill of staff and volunteer group leaders. Gradually, more of the courses are being accredited through the Open College network.

The nursery

The Pen Green nursery has 35 full time equivalent places, and six family workers, including the teacher who heads the team. Twenty per cent of the children are two-year-olds, and about half the children are now referred by health or social workers. The rest come from the local catchment area at the age of three, and usually stay for about a year before moving on to school. Staff say that it is 'vitally important' for all users that the nursery offers mainstream provision, and that it takes in families with a wide range of backgrounds, from affluent to breadline.

Most children come for four half-day sessions a week. A few stay for the full day, which ends at 3.30. The nursery is always oversubscribed, so Wednesday morning is kept for a drop-in for children and carers, giving those without places some access to the staff and facilities. On Wednesday afternoon, when the staff are engaged in meetings and development, a volunteer-led group for parents and under-fives use the premises. About 10 children regularly stay for a full nursery day, and others can always stay on occasion if there is a special reason. About 24 adults and children can stay for lunch – a civilised occasion which senior staff supervise while the rest take a short break.

Curriculum

The nursery's organisation and curriculum is a striking example of the way Pen Green staff have been ready to question, and sometimes overthrow, conventional professional practice to meet what they see as the needs of users – in this case, the children. Early on, the staff based the work fairly conventionally on themes such as 'growing', or 'size and shape'. But they found that 'the themes we spent so much time elaborating in staff meetings and building up as a staff group were largely irrelevant to the nursery children. They played on despite us, (Whalley 1994 page 52).

So they abandoned the themes, brought in even more sand, water, clay, peat and scrap materials, and watched children as they worked on their own concerns. Gradually they added more large boxes and crates, more stuff to make dens, more mirrors and real working objects. They say it was fairly chaotic at first, but gradually the workers became more experienced at observing children and helping to extend their individual play and interests. Then they discovered the work of an academic, Chris

Athey (Athey 1990), and its development by her colleague Tina Bruce, on 'schemas' – patterns of behaviour which, as the centre's booklet for parents puts it, can be 'puzzling or a pain in the neck'.

Some children may be 'transporting' – carrying things around, others 'connecting' – tying things together, or 'enveloping' – wrapping up themselves and everything else or posting things into video recorder slots. Children in a 'rotation' phase are fascinated by circles and things that turn and spin. 'Trajectory' is all about straight lines, jumping, sliding, streams of water, or pushing toys from A to B. The theory is that if nursery workers observe individual children's current 'schemas', they can successfully provide appropriate ideas and materials to extend their thinking and learning. 'We've become fascinated by how young children learn, and excited by it', said one family worker.

A lot of the materials in the nursery are everyday things like string, sellotape, labels and stickers. A great variety of materials are available all the time – paints and art materials, huge hollow blocks for building, a woodwork bench. There's a big outside area, with water on tap. The staff believe in working along with children's interests and self-chosen activities (Bruce, 1987, 1991). The aim is to develop children's autonomy, decision making, and ability to negotiate – all important attributes for success at school.

Most nursery workers share these aims. But at Pen Green, they seem to have been especially vigilant in cutting out adult-led routines that can interrupt children's extended play and thinking. They moved small group times for stories and discussions to the end of sessions, to minimise disruption of the children's play. Children can make themselves a snack of cereal, fruit or toast whenever they want at the attractive 'Pen Green café' in a corner of the nursery (Many parents make a small contribution of up to £1.50 each week to help cover the cost of the food).

It is a very warm and inviting nursery – staff regularly pick up children and hug them, parents wander round freely, and the café, the drapes used to lower ceilings, the two-story playhouse with real scaled down furniture (made by a father) and real kitchen and household utensils, and the intriguing natural objects lying around are very enticing for children. Parents who take part in groups looking at child development and learning sometimes make extra materials for the nursery, such as 'story sacks' children could borrow, with dolls and puppets and homemade pop up illustrations alongside a familiar book or story.

The children go on a lot of trips. Some even go on a short residential trip to a farm, without their parents. Both staff and parents were nervous at first, but staff take great care to find out about things like bedtime routines ('Bethany was allowed to have her bath and fall asleep on the sofa') and so far no child has wanted to be taken home early. There are still plenty of conventional activities, such as construction toys and puzzles and dominoes and the like. But they are produced unobtrusively when a child or member of staff wants them for an individual purpose. In a mainly white area, staff try to make sure that resources and activities reflect a multicultural society. They also place emphasis on aesthetic activities, such as art, dance and drama.

Some visitors in the early days thought that children were *too* free, and that free flow trajectory play with water just led to cold wet children. However the practice, and its underpinning systems and records (see *Observation, records and parent involvement* below) have developed a great deal in recent years, and the Pen Green nursery is very well regarded by local professionals. The main impression I received was of unusual warmth and satisfaction and enjoyment, both among children and between staff, and of a great deal of fruitful interaction between adults and children.

Not unusually, these days, the nursery includes some very angry and difficult children. It was noticeable how the children helped each other, coping with others' crying or tantrums with considerable skill. When one little girl was crying miserably, and clinging to a worker, another solved the problem by sticking her head out of a den made of drapes and saying welcomingly: 'This is a hospital but you can come in'.

Learning to be strong

Staff at Pen Green have developed a special curriculum to help children cope with threatening behaviour from either adults or other children. It started with parents' concern when a local child was abducted and abused, has constantly changed and developed over the years, and now reflects other issues, such as bullying and resolving conflict with friends. All four-year-olds (with parents' consent) take part in sessions run by workers they know well. The staff have special training for the programme with an outside consultant every year. Adults act out cautionary stories with dolls as props, and the children can then join in the role play, and try out different solutions.

The sessions cover bullying, conflict with friends, boundaries at home (for example, always asking an adult before going out to play with friends), and strangers (defined as 'someone who Mum or Dad doesn't know is talking to you'). A final session covers 'feelings' and includes the message that you never have to keep a secret if it feels wrong. In the role plays, the children practise shouting 'No' with an angry face, calling for help, and asking or telling adults when needed. They can also experiment with what may happen when they do not tell or shout in potentially dangerous situations. The programme seems highly valued by parents. 'It's done wonders for my daughter's confidence' said a father. There has been a lot of professional interest, and Pen Green staff now train others to undertake similar work.

Observation, records and parent involvement

The work of the nursery is based on systematic observation and recording of what children are doing. Every morning and afternoon there are two 'target' children, and all the family workers watch them and record what they do and say. In this way all children are regularly observed every few weeks. The child's family worker collects and summarises the observations, and analyses what 'schemas' the child is displaying. At their regular Monday meetings, the nursery staff use the observations to plan activities that will extend the child's learning and thinking and general well-being, and record the curriculum areas those activities will cover. They say that their knowledge of schemas helps them to introduce activities that will interest a child at a particular moment.

Staff also use a system for structured observation designed to measure children's well-being and involvement. 'It's a useful tool for discovering when things are going wrong in a child's life' said a worker. Family workers make home visits before the child comes in to the nursery, taking a pack which includes accessible information about the nursery, an entertaining booklet on schemas, and a pad and coloured pencils. There are further home visits at regular intervals – usually three visits altogether during the year most children spend in the nursery.

Family workers feed back the staff's observations to parents, and note children's interests at home. Many parents become fascinated by watching their children play and learn, and join in the planning by telling staff about children's interests, activities, and schemas at home. All the records of observations, action plans, curriculum coverage and home visits go into each child's 'Celebration of My Achievements' – a fat, loose-leaf file – along with drawings and pieces of work that children want to put in, and sometimes observations from parents. From the start, the intention was that all children's files should be open to parents and the children themselves. At first the records were filed in an office, and no one looked at them. Now they are available in filing drawers around the nursery, and are well used.

Special needs

Pen Green offers a variety of services for children with special needs and their parents. At the most informal level, parents of children with disabilities or other difficulties can come in and use some of the excellent facilities, such as the ball pool and Snoezelen room. Within the nursery, there is a 'nurture group' of four children who have been referred through social services. The children come in for two days a week, giving some respite to their families. Two sessional workers help to look after them.

One of the nursery family workers is the special needs coordinator, and when I was there the centre was applying for funding to extend her work to include outreach to schools and more groups and advocacy for parents. (She had already spent time counselling young children who were having difficulties in a local primary school.) She also runs the summer play scheme for children with special needs, which is integrated with the mainstream community play scheme but has its own staff and budget and space for children to withdraw from the crowd.

A 'closed' adult group helps to support parents of children with special needs. The centre staff often also provide support for parents who themselves have mental health problems or other special needs, and act as go-between with other services who can help them.

Research

Increasingly, staff at Pen Green have become involved in research. They were one of the pilot nurseries for Professor Chris Pascal's Effective Early Learning project, and gained a great deal from its emphasis on children's autonomy and concentration. In 1994 Margy Whalley spent 18 months at the Open University, returning in 1996 with the new title of Director of Research and Development: her deputy, Trevor Chandler, the centre's senior social worker, has remained acting head of the centre.

The centre has started two new research projects. One will focus on how children learn, and the role of parents and staff as educators. With the support of the Teacher Training Agency, staff and parents are making a CD-ROM of children playing and interacting with adults at home and in the nursery, and discussing and analysing the results. Parents working on the study take part in the selection and editing of material. Early in the project discussions of nursery workers' practice compared with what parents do at home had already proved enlightening.

The second study will investigate parents' views of the services available to them, and the support they need. Pen Green is training a group of parents in interview techniques, then paying them to do the field work: 'We think parents will be more forthcoming to other parents'. said Margy Whalley. Cath Arnold, the acting head of the nursery, has also been undertaking research with parents, investigating how children learn. All this activity means that some Pen Green parents become not just partners in their own children's education, but partners in deepening professional knowledge about children's learning, and how adults can promote it.

Multi-agency services

Other professionals in the area value the services at Pen Green highly. Several health visitors and a midwife take part in the centre's work, running groups and the clinic. A health visitor said: 'I try to get most families to come here, even if they don't live in the area. It's wonderful: the centre is for parents as people, as well as children. They can get their brains in gear.' Local social workers are less visible – the centre has two social workers on the staff, and those in the field are busy with crises and statutory child protection work. But the centre is an important resource for families receiving social services support.

The centre houses a legal advice project, and offers free pregnancy testing, family planning and counselling. 'It's not a clinical place, people get friendships going, there's a whole social aspect', said another health visitor. Other professionals, such as educational psychologists, speech therapists, and physiotherapists come in when they are needed, and run training sessions for staff.

Finance and management

The centre's main funding comes from Northamptonshire, with Education and Social Services splitting the annual £325,000 grant, mainly for salaries, down the middle. The Health Authority provides the equivalent of three days a week of health visitor time. The Social Services Department also provides extra money under Section 17 of the Children Act to help fund the creche, and pays for 15 places in the summer play scheme, and for sessional workers for the special needs nurture group.

The centre has a delegated budget. Its management is overseen by a policy group that meets quarterly. The committee includes representatives from the local education, health and social services authorities, two county councillors, and two elected parents. The senior staff bring in a consultant when needed to provide support and outside evaluation of their management. The centre raises extra funds for special projects, and has had money from the European Social Fund and charities. It holds very local fund-raising events for extras, such as trips for children and families, and small treats for children. The staff also raise income from professional conferences: Pen Green runs its own, highly successful conferences, and staff and users are often asked to contribute to outside conferences.

Outcomes

More than 300 families use Pen Green's services each week. At a cost of just over £1000 a year per family, the strength, confidence and educational boost both adults and children seem to gain from the centre seem to justify the spending. In significant numbers of cases the early support seems likely to prevent the need for future crisis spending by health, education and social services. Jan Rushton, the operations manager for social services in the area, who chairs the policy group, believes that the centre's 50 week a year provision for children, and its 'wholehearted involvement of parents in everything that goes on', have significant effects.

Surprisingly, given its socio-economic profile, Corby has the lowest number of children who have to be looked after by social services in the county: about 40, when the next lowest area has 65. 'Pen Green plays an important part in that', said Jan Rushton. However she believes the centre, though not in itself very expensive, would be very hard to replicate. Northamptonshire has other family centres, and is starting some family education projects to reach parents and young children – but they are not designed on anything like the scale of Pen Green.

Pen Green's influence has spread far beyond Northamptonshire. It has a stream of visitors from Britain and abroad, and has taken part in international projects. Others working in nursery centres, or thinking of starting one, have been inspired and revitalised by visits to Pen Green. Its development has benefited from the vision of local politicians, its fortunate location in a big empty school, the appointment of a charismatic leader who saw staff development and community participation as twin keys to success, and the commitment and campaigning energy of staff and parents. The result has become a very important model for others to use, and build on.

Box 11.2   Pen Green – summary

Strengths
- Listens to, and empowers, parents
- Very wide range of services for children and parents
- Education and training for adults
- Creates employment
- Multi-professional staff
- Excellent leadership and team building
- Use of consultants
- Enough time for quality planning and development
- Research and experiment

But
- Seen as expensive and difficult to replicate

---

12. The roots of success

The costs of neglect

At the end of 1996, Britain was reaching a state of near-panic about the upbringing of children. A head teacher had been murdered when trying to intervene in a fight. There were two much-publicised cases where the behaviour of a child, or a group of children, had brought schools to a standstill. The treatment of young offenders – and the costs of their crimes – had a high political profile, with politicians from both main parties advocating 'tough' punitive solutions.

Research showed that those offenders were very likely to have been excluded from school. Exclusions had rocketed in recent years to over 13,000. The number of children excluded from primary school had more than trebled, rising from 378 to 1445 – and a fifth of these were children excluded from reception classes. Researchers had found clear links between exclusions and unhappy childhoods, and between exclusion and poor levels of literacy.

According to a study for the Commission for Racial Equality, pupils permanently excluded from school cost education authorities £48 million – twice as much as children in school – but received just half a day's tuition a week for the price. (Parsons 1996). The risk factors leading to school exclusion and juvenile delinquency were widely agreed. A report for the Audit Commission, summing them up, included poor parenting, neglect, poor maternal and domestic care for under-fives, and the absence of a good relationship with at least one parent. Parents who used harsh punishment, or were erratic in their discipline, were twice as likely to have children in trouble (Perfect and Renshaw, 1996). David Farrington (1996) drew up a similar list, but included poverty as a factor. In 1995, 30 per cent of British babies were born into families receiving state benefits because of poverty.

These reports into the prevention of criminality suggested that school failure and juvenile offending could be tackled at their roots by:

- parent education and pre-natal advice to parents on diet and child care;

- high quality pre-school education;
- programmes to help young children with impulsive and aggressive behaviour.

Most of the centres in this book offer all these things in a way that is well accepted and appreciated by parents.

The numbers of children with statements of special educational needs had also risen sharply, with a two thirds rise since 1986, and the curve still upwards. For instance, 1994-95 saw a 13 per cent increase. Three per cent of school age children now had statements. Department for Education and Employment figures estimated that catering for special needs was costing local authorities £2.5 billion, or 12.5 per cent of their education budget.

There were particular concerns among primary teachers and health visitors about the behaviour problems of very young children in nursery and reception classes. Nursery teachers reported increasing numbers of children who did not know how to play, and whose behaviour was chaotic and fragmented. In Bradford, for example, there had been a 20 per cent increase in referrals of children under five to educational psychologists (Williams 1996). Department of Health statistics showed a 25 per cent rise in children needing psychiatric help between 1986 and 1991.

Increasing numbers of children were being diagnosed as having Attention Deficit Disorder or hyperactivity (or both). Parents of such children complained on chat-shows that they had recognised problems when their children were still very young, and tried to get professional help. But no one took their difficulties seriously until the children started to cause trouble in school.

Not surprisingly, professionals in services that were supposed to help deal with all these problems were very over-stretched. Social workers were mostly too tied up with the child protection aspects of the Children Act to have enough time to take the Act's preventive measures seriously. Educational psychologists were swamped with referrals, and spent much of their time drawing up statements of special educational needs, rather than working with teachers on preventive measures. Health visitors had less time for home visiting and preventive work with families in need.

The potential of early years centres

The case for multi-agency services, designed to identify parents in difficulties as early as possible in their children's lives, get alongside them, and work in partnership with them to make sure that children are given quality care and educational stimulus from the time they are born, is now very strong indeed. Early intervention can save money on crisis and remedial intervention when problems have become deep-rooted.

More positively, every literacy problem that is prevented by early intervention, every behaviour problem that is sorted out at an early age, every parent that can be helped to get on well with his or her young children, to enjoy their childhood, and to promote their healthy development, will represent an enormous gain in both children's and parents' happiness, self-esteem, and achievement.

It is crucial to the success of multi-agency early years centres that they also support, educate, and help to address the problems of ordinary coping families. Needs are growing for them too. The proportion of mothers with children under five working full time has gone up from five per cent in 1983 to 16 per cent in 1995. In the same period the proportion working part time was up from 18 per cent to 32 per cent. Neighbourhood early childhood centres can offer support and access to training to a range of people working with young children, including childminders. They can also provide high quality, educational out-of school and holiday care for primary school children.

Some of these coping families have particular needs. Children of recent immigrants will succeed faster in education if they and their parents can have skilled help with English when the children are young. Children in families who live in poverty and cramped housing will thrive on good space and equipment for physical and exploratory play. Children with behaviour problems can improve out of recognition when their parents have early advice and support. So can children with developmental delay or learning disabilities. Open-access early years centres, with clear and effective equal opportunities policies, are geared to respond to the needs of parents and children from the time the children are born.

No single service or institution will magically remove all future problems. Too many factors come together to create expensive difficulties – poor housing and environment; conflicts between parents and partners; poverty; peer group influences; inadequate schools; a child's own genetic make-up. But any service that can greatly reduce the numbers of cases needing expensive crisis intervention will give health and social workers and teachers much more time for the severe cases that early intervention cannot prevent.

Prevention can pay for itself quite quickly. The cost of a child 'looked after' by social services was £34,000 in 1994 (Pugh and others, 1994). So if the work of an early childhood centre keeps just one child out of care each year, the saving will cover the salary and costs of a social worker employed at that centre. The evidence of social workers interviewed in this study suggests that centres can have a marked effect in reducing the numbers of 'looked after' children in their areas. As one said: 'the only way of freeing a few social workers from the child protection juggernaut is to attach them to this kind of project (see Chapter 5, Greengables, *Future prospects*).

A similar calculation could be made of the savings that early prevention of literacy and behaviour problems would make on education budgets. Primary heads who take children from some of the early years centres in this study say that they have not seen the big rise in numbers of children with special needs that has affected the work and budgets of many schools.

A well-known longitudinal study in the United States followed the progress of very disadvantaged children who went through a high-quality pre-school programme, and compared them with a matched control group. The Perry pre-school project in Ypsilanti, Michigan (which originated the High/Scope curriculum approach) consisted of nursery education with specially trained staff, and – perhaps crucially – a great deal of parent involvement.

The research found that 71 per cent of the High/Scope children completed high school, compared with 54 per cent of the others. At the age of 27, 59 per cent of the High/Scope group had received state benefits compared with 80 per cent of the control group. Seven per cent had been arrested five or more times, compared with 35 per cent. The researchers calculated that for every $1000 invested in the pre-school programme, savings from the costs of remedial education, delinquency, income support, joblessness and tax gains brought back $7160 (Schweinhart and Weikart, 1993).

Early years centres promote parents' confidence and knowledge of the part they themselves can play in their children's education from birth onwards. Parents' suspicion – or hostility – towards schools changes to a culture where they see themselves as partners in their children's education. This is particularly important when the parent's own experience is of school failure and unhappiness.

Larger centres can provide high-quality day care and education for the children of parents who are working, or studying, or under stress. They can help parents over the short-term crises that can affect any family. They give parents opportunities for further education and training, helping them out of poverty, welfare and unemployment, as well as removing the consequences to their children of very low self-esteem. They deliver health and social services in an accessible and acceptable way, and are well placed, when necessary, to bring parents into contact with more specialised support in a non-threatening way.

Those benefits are now well known, and well agreed. What the many official reports praising the work of such centres do not convey is the life-enhancing qualities of good early years centres: the sense of community; the jokes; the mutual support parents offer each other; the cheerful and open relations between staff, children and parents; the independence and confidence of children; and the interest, satisfaction and enjoyment of staff in the job they are doing, however worrying and stressful the work can often be. As the Hillfields mother, whose husband wanted her to move out of the area on the grounds it was 'only a nursery' said: 'It's not just a nursery. It's our life.'

Key factors

The centres in this study had a variety of aims and services. Even so it is possible to draw some general conclusions about key factors that make for success.

Open access

It is essential to the success of the centres that they are open to all families in their local area, and take a mix of 'mainstream' local families and those 'in need', referred by social services or health workers because they have problems. One commentator has said that community-based open access services 'allow reciprocity to thrive, and the range of coping abilities among families using the centres allows them to support each other (and their community) rather than merely be the recipients of services' (Statham, 1994). The Audit Commission, in its report on coordinating child health and social services for children in need, concluded that a mix of open access with a quota of referred families is preferable to a closed system (Audit Commission 1994)

There are several drawbacks to 'closed' services, limited to children and parents identified by professionals as having particular needs. One is the stigma attached to referral. If services are clearly designed for families in difficulties, as are most social services family centres, parent may well be resentful about referral. The father at the Netherton Park family centre was a good example of someone who had rejected 'stigmatised' help – but was happy with counselling and support that was clearly part of a mainstream service (see Chapter 4, *Family support*).

A second drawback is that any system for referral will miss families who have considerable needs, but do not happen to come to the attention of professionals. When Manchester opened new open-access family centres, they found that several families whose children were given 'mainstream' day care places just because they lived in the catchment area turned out to have equally high, if not higher, levels of need as the families given places because they met the criteria used to allocate places in social services day nurseries. (Smith 1996.)

'Closed' services can also lower expectations of what children can achieve in high-quality nursery provision. In centres such as Sandal Agbrigg and Dorothy Gardner, which had started with fairly separate 'social services' and 'education' sections, workers said that mixing children from families in need with the others had greatly raised their own expectations of what two to four-year-olds could achieve. And the children themselves had a much wider range of peers to lead them into productive and challenging activities.

Parent involvement and support

A nursery or day care programme that works only with children cannot have much impact on the homes where children spend most of their lives. A key element in any effective pre-school programme must be increasing parents' understanding and knowledge about their children's development and education, and helping to build the self-esteem and confidence of demoralised, depressed or defensive parents.

The most effective pre-school programmes are 'powerful in engineering, reinforcing and sustaining parental aspirations and interest in their children's education' (Woodhead 1985). One noticeable feature of the original High/Scope programme, which producedsuch impressive outcomes, was that it included frequent and extended home visits by trained workers to every parent in the programme.

Neighbourhood early years centres are an ideal place to involve parents, and get them interested in – and excited by – their children's learning. They are very accessible. Both staff and parents have time to spend talking informally about children's interests and progress. When special needs have been identified, professionals such as speech therapists can involve parents in a therapeutic programme more easily when they meet them in a setting that is accessible, familiar and comfortable, and where staff can back up their work from week to week.

Parents who may find it difficult to get to a special clinic will regularly attend sessions at a local centre. Social workers merged into a multi-professional team can provide very acceptable early support. It is easy for nursery workers to alert them to a family who may be in trouble, when a formal referral to the local social work team would not seem appropriate.

Centres do not have to offer structured 'parent education'. Many parents prefer informal advice, as and when they need it, provided the advice takes account of their own skills and knowledge and culture (Pugh and others, 1994). In an open-access centre, it is easy to offer acceptable advice about parents' immediate concerns – often problems about behaviour, sleep, feeding and toilet training. When a group of parents shares particular problems, as they often do, it is relevant, and acceptable, for staff to suggest that a group might meet and discuss these issues with professionals such as health visitors.

The workers can unobtrusively demonstrate good ways of encouraging children's language development, good behaviour, and enjoyment of learning. Both in the lunches and snacks they provide, and in cookery groups with children and adults, workers can informally introduce the principles of healthy eating.

Helping parents to handle the everyday problems of toddlerhood, such as tantrums and attention-seeking, can have a disproportionate effect on children's happiness and development. A child's day is made up of small things, and adults' response to those small things makes a big difference, as anyone watching parents and toddlers in a supermarket can quickly see. As a mother at Robinswood said: 'Children and parents both need this sort of a place. Children learn to play with each other. And if I didn't have this place, I'd be belting him at the end of the day.'

Adult education and training

Some parents also welcome accessible daytime education and training opportunities for themselves. Many are tied to the school hours of older children. They say they just cannot use services that involve the time and expense of bus rides. Centres that offer a range of opportunities for adults can have a big impact on parents' self-confidence and eventually on their earning (and tax-paying) potential.

They are places where parents come anyway, to take advantage of services for their children, and where it is easy for them to make new friends. Once there, and comfortable, they are much readier to take up any opportunities on offer. Several parents at centres in this study also stressed how important it was to know that their children would be well looked after, by familiar and qualified staff, when they were at groups and classes.

Examples from this study show what a big range of opportunities early years centres can offer. Some increase parents' enjoyment in bringing up children, such as baby massage, or groups discussing aspects of child development and early years curriculum. Some respond to parents' own interests and help to make the centres warm, civilised and cheerful places, such as aromatherapy and sewing and cooking (see, for example, the adult education provided at Greengables, Chapter 5, *The New Building*).

Many parents move on from informal groups to more formal adult education and training at the centres or at local colleges. Centres in the study offered basic literacy programmes, computer and information technology courses, NVQs in child care, GCSE and A level courses, access course for further and higher education, foreign language classes, and Open University programmes. All these opportunities clearly do a great deal to build parents' self-respect and develop positive attitudes and confidence that they too can learn and develop. Their new attitudes have a knock-on effect on their children's happiness and development.

Finally, early years centres offer a few parents the experience of taking part in the management of an institution they know very well, and where they feel comfortable Participation in management leads parents who would once never have dreamed of themselves in the role to become school governors and comminity leaders.

Under threes

The best time of all to get alongside parents – the time when they are most available, and open to support and advice – is when their children are babies and toddlers. It is remarkable that in Britain, the debate about nursery education has for many years focused entirely on three- and four-year-olds. In France, in contrast, nearly 52 per cent of two-year-olds were in nursery schools in 1994. One large-scale longitudinal study found that those who had entered the écoles maternelles as two-year-olds were level pegging with those who started nursery school at three. But the two-year-old nursery children had moved significantly ahead in mathematics and French by the time they seven (Jarousse and others, 1992).

Centres that combine child care and nursery education are well placed to offer a good early educational start for under three, and not only for the children who have day care places and come on their own, but for children who come with parents or minders. Some centres in this study have developed a well-planned curriculum for babies and toddlers, based on knowledge of child development, and building on close observation of individual children's interests and activities. Many parents at such centres have become fascinated by their babies' and toddlers' learning. Patterns of behaviour that can madden parents become much more tolerable, and even interesting, when they are seen as a stage in a child's learning. Early intervention becomes crucial when children have disabilities or special needs. The earlier needs are identified, the easier it is to provide good support for parents, suggesting activities and approaches that will promote the best personal and educational outcomes for the child. In many cases, this early intervention will enable the child to succeed in mainstream education.

Continuity for children

The lack of day care and nursery facilities in Britain has meant that young children face a great deal of change, at an age when they most need stability. Many young children can move from parent to minder to creche to playgroup to nursery to reception class, all within the first four years of their lives. Some have two or three changes of carer each day. If older schoolchildren were expected to make so many rapid moves, there would be a national outcry. The early years centres provide one familiar place, with familiar workers, where children can start by coming with their parents, and gradually be left on their own. They can be cared for over families' short-term crises, and their hours are often flexible enough to suit working parents.

Responding to local needs

Policy makers should not make too many prior assumptions about the services parents need. Different neighbourhoods have different requirements, depending on employment patterns, cultural traditions, and many other factors – and those requirements change over time, as at Hillfields (Chapter 2, *Introduction*). Birmingham, when planning new 'wraparound' pre-school services based in primary schools, found that many parents wanted informal groups and advice and congenial meeting places rather than day care (Birmingham City Council, 1996).

A study of single parents with young children found that only one in seven of those without jobs said that lack of affordable child care was the sole barrier to them working. Forty-two per cent said their main reason for not working was that they felt their children were too young, and needed their mothers at home (Ford 1996). Neighbourhood children's centres offering further education and training are ideal for such parents.

It was noticeable that centres with a multi-ethnic staff in a multi-ethnic area, such as Patmore and Hillfields, had a special ethos. Parents from minority backgrounds were particularly comfortable, and, at Hillfields, the arrival of several bilingual workers had attracted new parents to the centre. One centre, Pen Green (Chapter 11), had also set out to recruit male staff, and this had helped to bring fathers into the centre, as well as providing good role models for boys.

Nursery curriculum and organisation

Most state nursery education in this country now takes place in nursery classes attached to primary schools. However, about 85 per cent of four-year-olds are not even in nursery classes, but in reception classes designed primarily for children aged five. A survey of 2000 early years establishments catering for children under five in 1994 found that only a quarter of teachers had appropriate training for early years education (Blenkin and Yue, 1994).

Early years centres, with large and varied staff teams, are particularly well placed to develop a high quality nursery curriculum, and take advantage of recent research into children's learning and development. Their range of services for under-threes and parents, and for parents on their own, brings opportunities for fresh thinking about curriculum, and for genuine parent involvement in curriculum development. The work with younger children helps them to build their curriculum from the bottom up rather than from the national curriculum down, making sure that inappropriate pressures do not cramp the development of three and four-year-olds. It is much harder for a lone nursery class teacher, let alone a reception class teacher, to resist these pressures.

There has been increasing knowledge and concern in recent years about the effects of inappropriate demands on four-year-olds, particularly, but not exclusively, those in reception classes (see for example Pugh 1996b). The School Curriculum and Assessment Authority guidelines for nursery curriculum, *Desirable Outcomes* (DfEE/SCAA 1996) have not really addressed this danger. Their emphasis on very early acquisition of specific academic competences needs careful interpretation if it is not to lead to practice that will constrict young children's development (including their cognitive development), rather than promote it.

An earlier Government report, from the 1990 Rumbold Committee into the quality of education of three- to five-year-olds, seemed well aware of these dangers, saying of nursery professionals: 'It is within their power to encourage feelings of fun and discovery in learning on the one hand, or of dull drudgery on the other. Particular attention has to be given in these early years to the process by which a child acquires the disposition to learn and necessary competencies for learning' (DES 1990. The report warned that 'educators should guard against pressure which might lead them to over-concentration on formal teaching and on attainment of specific targets'

The most sophisticated research into the long-term outcomes of nursery education has been done in the United States. The conclusion from a number of high-quality nursery programmes relate to 'life skills' rather than specific cognitive gains. The most important impact of early education appears to be on children's self-esteem, motivation, and commitment to school (Rutter 1985, Sylva 1994). Nursery centres can multiply these effects by promoting parents' as well as children's self-esteem and life skills.

It was noticeable that most of the centres in this study, had recently made changes in their curriculum planning and organisation for three- and four-year-olds, in order to give children more choices and independence in their play and work. This change was intended to promote the confidence, skills, concentration and positive attitudes likely to help children most when they went to school.

Adult-led group activities were guided by close observation and analysis of children's chosen activities and persistent interests, and designed to meet their individual needs. The result seemed to be very confident, articulate and independent children, many of whom concentrated for long periods on self-imposed tasks, and contributed well to group activities. Parents were knowledgeable about their children's progress in different areas, and involved in strategies to take the children forward. These attributes boded well for the children's progress through school.

Promoting sociable behaviour

One of the most striking things about early years centres, particularly in their work with children under three, is the way the help to socialise children, and involve parents in their socialisation.   Encouraging a group of one- and two-year-olds to sit happily round a table having lunch or a snack, or to join in group activities and discussions, may well be as important for their future success at school as intense early emphasis on colours, shapes, letters and numbers – the main stuff of nursery education in the eyes of many parents, and, it sometimes seems, government policy makers.

Good nursery centres have effective policies on dealing with difficult behaviour and bullying, and encouraging sharing and mutual help, from the time children are very young. Just as important, parents come to understand good strategies for handling difficult and anti-social behaviour. A child who goes on to school comfortable in groups, and knowing the standards of manners and behaviour expected by teachers, will have a big head start over a child who has to learn those things at the age of four or five in a large reception class, usually causing a good deal of disruption to other children's learning.

Outreach

There will always be parents who are too stressed, or shy, or depressed, to bring children even to a very local and welcoming centre of their own accord. Outreach is an important part of the work of several of the centres in this study. Centres with social workers on the staff, or those that have developed their nursery nurses skills as 'family workers', are well placed to go out to families and support them in their homes.

Outreach does not only extend to families. Centres can support other services in the neighbourhood – playgroups, parent and toddler groups and drop-ins, childminders. They can share their facilities and training sessions with other groups, and form a central base for a local early years forum. Many of the centres in this study were also centres for training for National Vocational Qualifications (NVQs) in child care, offering accredited training to childminders and classroom assistants in infant schools. Some offered a training base for Pre-school Learning Alliance courses for playgroup leaders.

Centres can also provide excellent facilities for community groups concerned with children, such as Portage, or groups from a particular ethnic minority, or self-managing groups of childminders. All these links can enrich and inform local work with children, inside and outside the centre, and make for higher quality all round.

Leadership

Leading a multi-agency centre is not an easy job. Without strong leadership, staff with different professional backgrounds and different pay and conditions of service, can generate friction and internal tensions. Multi-agency centres do not fit into normal bureaucratic categories. Joint funding can double up bureaucratic checks and routines. Increasingly, centre's managers are having to raise funds themselves for new projects, or even to keep their core services going.

The most effective leaders had two outstanding characteristics. First, they set out to provide services that their local parents and users wanted (see, for example, the starting points for the Netherton Family Centre, Greengables, and Pen Green, Chapters 4, 5 and 11). Second, they put a great deal of energy into team-building and staff development. Provided leaders are given real managerial control (preferably with a delegated budget), adequate administrative support, and a supportive line manager who understands the aims and scope of the enterprise, the job is clearly a very rewarding one.

Heads of early years centres also have their own professional network in the National Association of Nursery Centres. Many of the heads in this study, and their colleagues, are regular contributors to early years training courses. Several took part in a project which is producing training materials to support early years managers. (Whalley and others, in press.)

Staff development and training

All the well-established centres in the study had developed a strong culture of in-service training and review. Most have five full days for staff in-service training each year. Several also shut early one day a week for staff meetings, record-keeping, and training. In addition, many centres encouraged their staff to take individual training courses, and helped by paying fees and giving some time off for study. The varied needs of the job led to workers taking part in a great variety of training, ranging from higher degrees to counselling.

This culture of training and improvement is essential to the development of high quality services. The great majority of staff are nursery nurses, many of whom left school at 16 and then took a two-year training course. Creches and after school schemes may be staffed by parents or others who come in to the work with little or no training of any kind (though they may have considerable experience of children). The job can be a very stressful one. Visiting many of the centres in this study, one quickly becomes aware of its demands. Staff whose training concentrated on normal child development are in the front line dealing with parents' suicide threats and mental illness, as well as some very disturbed children.

Offering adequate non-contact time for staff development makes for a very cost-effective service. With good training and support, nursery nurses in some centres (for example Sandal Agbrigg, Hillfields and Netherton) were taking on complex family support work. In others, such as Patmore, they were leading curriculum development and change.

In multi-agency centres, with contributions from health, education and social services, staff can take advantage of in-service training opportunities provided by all three services. Centres with strong voluntary sector links have a further source of training opportunities, offering yet another perspective. Some of the larger centres, such as Pen Green, Hillfields and Dorothy Gardner, had also benefited from working closely with academics specialising in early childhood education, management consultants, and other outsiders. Sometimes these consultants also ran sessions for parents.

This culture of review and development, and the resulting professional confidence and skill of the centres' workers, made them excellent training bases for a variety of students whose work will bring them in contact with young children and parents. Most of the centres in the study provided practical training for student nursery nurses and teachers, and some also took social work, medical, and nursing students. Staff in several centres also played a wider part in the in-service training of other professionals within their local authority and elsewhere, offering expertise in areas such as nursery curriculum development, special needs, child protection and risk assessment, bilingual support, and equal opportunities.

Costs and funding

It is difficult to disentangle the full costs of all the centres in this study. Their running costs often come from several different pockets – local education, health and social services authorities; charities and trusts; money from Urban Aid or the European Social Fund. Extra contributions come from the education GEST budget for in-service training; from Section 19 of the Children Act for social services preventive work for children 'in need'; from Training and Enterprise Councils; and from Section 11 of the Local Government Act for work with ethnic minorities.

The cost of centres depends on a number of factors: the needs of the neighbourhood; the range of services on offer; the numbers of children on roll (and particularly the number of under-threes, who require higher staffing ratios); the number of teachers and social workers on the staff; the hours of opening, and whether services run all year round, or only in term-time. Some centres charged fees for some services. At Patmore, parents paid for day care places on a sliding scale linked to their income: fee income at Patmore brought in £55,000. Several centres charged for playgroups and parent and toddler groups, and for holiday and out-of-school care.

The newer centres were often hampered by the tendency of Government and voluntary agencies to underestimate the time it takes to develop a new service to a stage where it can begin to cover its costs. Recently, the trend has been to fund three-year pilot schemes at best, and often to offer funding only for one or two years. This kind of time-scale is too short to establish a demand and set up a good infrastructure to meet it. The babysitting exchange at the Patmore Centre (Chapter 3, *Community development*) is a good example of an excellent project with one-year funding that needed more time.

At the time of writing, the future of one centre, Patmore, looked very precarious, due to Save the Children's diminished resources and changed priorities. The ACE centre in Oxfordshire, partly funded by a three year Rural Development Commission grant, which was just ending, also looked insecure, since Oxfordshire was facing severe funding cuts. Greengables in Edinburgh was depending on its Urban Aid grant being renewed for a further period, or its local council finding extra money, to continue its valuable new services for parents and adults.

A key difficulty when trying to calculate the value for money offered by different centres is that there are no appropriate points of comparison. The Audit Commission has calculated the costs per hour of different services for under-fives in a London borough as 99p for a playgroup, £1.04 for a four year old in a reception class, £1.91 for a nursery class, and £24.04 for a home visiting scheme (Audit Commission 1996).

But this kind of calculation says little about the costs and benefits of combined centres that offer a range of linked services, including education for children under three, social services family support, community health services, therapy for children with special needs, and adult education and training. Nor does it allow for savings when such services, working together, prevent future spending on special needs, mental health, welfare benefits, child protection and the like, and boost participation in education, training, and ultimately employment and tax-paying.

Two studies by Sally Holterman (1992 and 1995) argued that a combined package of free nursery education for three- and four-year-olds, together with subsidised day care which parents would pay for according to their means, would add £2.7 billion to public expenditure. However, the income tax and national insurance contributions of women coming off benefit would, over time, more than cover that expenditure.

It would take a study of the long-term outcomes for children and families using multi-agency centres to prove in a UK context that good services for young children and their parents result in public expenditure savings. But the comparatively low numbers of child protection cases and of children with expensive behaviour and learning difficulties in areas with well-established under fives centres are suggestive. And there is plenty of anecdotal evidence from parents who have benefited from the services, and from health visitors, social workers and primary head teachers, about the preventive effects of centres.

Real and perceived blocks to replication

Money

The biggest block to opening new multi-agency centres is their apparent cost. It was encouraging that two of the centres in this study had opened within the last three years. The Netherton Family Centre (Chapter 4), and the ACE Centre (Chapter 10), show that where there is leadership on the ground, support from a local authority, and when funding partners can be found, it is still possible to set up new multi-agency services to meet the needs of parents and young children.

However local authorities with a successful centre had not felt able to replicate it elsewhere. As one social worker said, sadly: 'It shouldn't be special. Every school ought to be able to provide child care for parents who need to return to work, and to have good facilities for parents to come in and help along their children's education, and their own'.

Different pay and conditions for staff

Some local authorities have fought shy of multi-agency centres because of the complications of employing staff on different pay and conditions in the same institution. In other places professionals and their unions have resisted new flexible or extended contracts. But in practice, when a centre is going well it is inundated with applications for jobs. Staff know the score when they join a centre, and enjoy the variety and challenge of the work, and the range of opportunities for training and development. Almost all the centres in the study had very stable staffing. Workers, whether teachers, nursery nurses or social workers, said it was difficult to move on because other jobs in the field were so much more limited, and less interesting.

Local authority and national structures

A local authority's structure for delivering pre-school services appears to have surprisingly little impact on services on the ground. One study compared three types of local authority organisation. One group had integrated their services for under eights, setting up a joint committee or subcommittee of the education and social services committees, with substantial delegated powers. Another group had coordinated services, with significant formal arrangements between departments at council-lor and officer level. Finally, one authority had few formal arrangements beyond normal management procedures.

In all the authorities, circumstances beyond their control, such as budget cuts, or the pressure for a single date of admission to primary schools, made it very difficult to plan rationally across all services. The type of organisation, whether integrated or coordinated, did not seem to affect the quality of policy making or the ability to resist external pres-sures. Nor did it help to bridge the unhelpful boundaries between day care services and child protection and family support. The authors con-cluded: 'Structures are important, but so too are relationships between key individuals who must be able to transcend the barriers of profes-sional jealousies and vested interests and work openly together in the best interests of children and their parents' (Pugh and McQuail 1995, p.16).

Integration still has to take place in the teeth of continuing divisions between services at national level. Child care, nursery education, family support, and child health services are treated as different entities. All the authorities in the survey claimed to be trying to bring coherence to services for young children, but said they were hampered by the lack of a clear lead from the government departments most closely concerned.

Government initiatives that should have led to better coordination – such as the Section 19 reviews under the Children Act and the Depart-ment of Health Children's Services Plans – have often done little more than describe current provision, according to recent Audit Commission reports. They have not related that provision to an analysis of needs and resources (Audit Commission 1996). But they are still there to be used. Dudley's Section 19 review provided the justification for setting up the Netherton Family Centre, and determined the shape of its services (Chapter 4).

And excellent cooperation can be achieved at a very local level, as the arrangements between Robinswood and its host school show. It just needs people who say, as the Robinswood primary school head said: 'We're all in the same business, providing for local children and families. There's no place for empire builders and ego trips' – and then take action to prove they mean it.

Piecemeal regulation and the market culture

More recently, the market culture that has been imposed on the provi-sion of services has militated against planning and integration. Even in local authorities with merged or coordinated services for young children, the new requirements and pressures on the health, educational and social services, imposed piecemeal by central government has made genuine coordination difficult.

Some of the centres were facing inspection by three separate agencies – regular OFSTED inspections of nursery education, new 'light touch' inspections for nursery providers taking vouchers, and social services inspections of day care provision. None of these inspections was set up to evaluate what the centres are trying to do in their preventive work with parents and children. Health visitors now employed by GP practices said the work they did running groups and clinics in a centre was becoming increasingly difficult to justify to their employers, who were interested only in their own list of patients.

Nursery vouchers and early admission to primary school

The nursery voucher initiative, due to start nationally in April 1997, will make the development of integrated services even more difficult. The scheme (which gives all parents of four-year olds a voucher worth £1,100 to spend on part-time nursery education) only affects part-time nursery education for four-year-olds. Instead of encouraging support networks between schools, nurseries, and playgroups it sets them against each other in competition for customers. The voucher income is supposed to cover staff training, and provides no additional money for special needs.

Research by the National Children's Bureau into the impact of vouchers in four pilot areas found that the scheme did more to push children into reception classes than to expand nursery education. Playgroups, in particular, lost out. Vouchers also imposed a burden of time-consuming administration on nurseries (Pugh and Owen, 1996). The scheme carries its own high national administrative costs, further reducing money available for young children, and will support the private sector at the expense of targeting resources to the most needy children and families.

Even without a voucher scheme, many of the centres in the study were losing four-year-olds to nursery and reception classes in local primary schools. Several parents said that the centre's staffing ratios, appropriate curriculum, and flexible hours suited both their children and themselves better than primary school classes. But they felt pressured to secure a place at the school of their choice as early as possible. Voucher income will make schools more insistent that parents take up places early.

The scheme could affect the centres' in other ways. All centres taking vouchers will have to provide five two and a half hour sessions a week in term-time to qualify for vouchers. Several of the nursery centres in this study offered a mixture of all-day and half day sessions, to fit parents' and children's needs, and extend their services to the maximum number of children. Some offered year-round care and education. The voucher scheme would provide no income for this kind of flexible approach. The scheme will undoubtedly make planning, coordination, and provision for younger pre-school children and their parents even more difficult.

Training

Appropriate training for workers with young children and their parents is still very thin on the ground. Early Childhood Studies integrated degrees, now running in about ten universities, are a good start (Pugh 1996c). But training for nursery nurses is still fragmented between a variety of courses. National Vocational Qualifications in child care have added another qualification, rather than helping to standardise training. The expected NVQ Level Four qualification, which could provide a ladder for the holders of lower-level nursery and child care qualifications, has still not been developed.

Visions and prospects

By 1996 the trends in pre-school provision were as follows:

- a slow increase in part-time nursery education;
- growing numbers of four-year-olds in reception classes;
- a substantial increase in private day care for well-educated, high-earning women;
- a great shortage of day care, out of school and holiday provision.

Services in Britain, in contrast with those in other European countries, were characterised by:

- low levels of public funding;
- growing reliance on the private and voluntary sectors;
- little parental choice: demand outstrips supply;
- uncoordinated services, run by different departments at local and national level;
- services based on different ideologies, with different aims and purposes, and with different hours, admission criteria, charges, staff training, pay and conditions.

The Rumbold report concluded in 1990 that 'the achievement of better coordination [of services for under-fives] would be greatly helped if central government gave a clear lead, setting a national framework within which local development could take place' (DES 1990). Labour party policy, announced in 1996, could provide that lead. It will require local authorities to draw up an early years development plan for the care and education of children.

It promises a new framework of qualifications that would break down professional divides between workers with under-fives, and provide career development through a 'climbing frame' of qualifications

(Labour, 1996) Labour would concentrate policy-making for under fives in one government department, the Department for Education and Employment. On the education side, Labour announced it would scrap the nursery voucher scheme and review the targets set in *Desirable Outcomes*.

Labour has recognised the value of multi-agency centres. It has said that it would set up Early Excellence Centres in 25 regions, offering integrated early education and care. (The education would be free, the child care based on parents' ability to pay.) The centres would have at least 75 places for children, two thirds of them three- to five-year-olds, and would include other services such as drop-ins for parents, health services, outreach, and toy libraries. Their results would be evaluated.

These policies would constitute a big step forward, provided they built on the experience of existing initiatives and services, responded to local communities' needs rather than imposing a standard blueprint, and set out to create and support local cooperative networks of providers and improve quality all round. The policy reflects the vision of integrated early childhood services that a number of people and agencies have put forward in recent years.

There is now considerable agreement among professionals and those interested in early years care, education and family support about the shape of appropriate services for young children and parents. That was not always the case. For many years early years lobbies fought each other: advocates of voluntary playgroups ranged themselves against advocates of state nursery education, and proponents of good affordable day care for working mothers opposed both kinds of nursery educator.

However in the 1990s all parties managed to come together and, with some difficulty, to find a more unified voice. The Early Childhood Education Forum brought together 45 organisations involved in nursery education and child care. In 1994 the Forum published a vision for early childhood care and education (Duffy and Griffin, 1994). Most people working in the field – and all the parents who benefit from centres such as those in this study – would subscribe to this vision.

The starting aim is to provide year-round, high-quality, fully integrated care and education for young children, working in partnership with parents. Local centres and networks should be based on existing provision in the statutory, voluntary and private sectors, including primary schools. Services would vary, depending on the expressed needs of the local community. They should always be open to all families; offer flexible patterns of provision and attendance; and reflect diversity and actively counter all discrimination.

The network would provide both centre-based provision and family day care in the homes of childminders recruited, trained, supported and monitored by the centre. The centres would also provide a range of facilities, on the lines of the bigger centres in this study – drop-ins, toy libraries, health clinics, groups and training for adults (and staff), home visiting and access to other professionals.

They would arrange after school and holiday care, and provide information and individual support for parents, and meeting places for community groups. All services for children would be based on partnership with parents, and the recognition that parents are experts in their own child's needs and development, and that different child rearing practices and patterns of family life can all succeed well for children. Such services would require a coherent national policy for early childhood care and education, with an appropriate legislative framework and financial support. There would need to be established national standards, and appropriate training.

At present, nursery services are a long way from that point. Most parents have very little in the way of advice and support before children become three. Between the ages of three and five, children with working parents often have what has been described as a period marked by frequent change and discontinuity, rather than the three-year period of nursery schooling found in most other European countries (Moss and Pen,1996).

There is now a great deal of evidence from centres in this study, and others like them, that such services can bring great benefits to parents and children, particularly in areas with large numbers of parents living in poverty. At present the way in which Britain organises – or fails to organise – pre-school services does almost nothing to support parents of children under three, to interest them in their children's education, and to offer services that meet their needs. This is particularly critical when it comes to the identification and early support of parents and children with special needs.

Parents of children over three are faced with a limited range of part-time education services of very variable quality. Many of the teachers working with young children lack appropriate training. For working parents, and those who need or want work or education and training, there is inadequate day care provision, and much of it has no direct educational input.

For many years now there have been successful models for integrated services that provide the flexible services parents require, support them in the upbringing and education of their young children and, in many cases, remove the need for later expensive crisis intervention when educational and social problems have taken root.

The national panic about educational standards and the upbringing and behaviour of young people has led to a great deal of public hand-wringing about the inadequacies of modern parents and family life. What we need now is the political will to use the well-established experience of integrated early years centres, and to build services that support parents and promote children's learning and development throughout the critical years from birth to five, when the foundations of children's later success and happiness, at school and in life, are laid down.

References

Athey, C (1990) *Extending Thought in Young Children.* Paul Chapman.

Audit Commission (1994) *Seen but not Heard: coordinating Community Child Health and Social Services for Children in Need: Executive Summary.* The Audit Commission.

Audit Commission (1996) *Counting to Five: Education of Children Under Five.* The Audit Commission.

Audit Commission (1996) *Under-fives Count: A Management Handbook on the education of Children Under Five.* The Audit Commission

Ball, C (1994) *Start Right: The Importance of Early Learning.* Royal Society for the Encouragement of Arts, Manufactures and Commerce (RSA).

Birmingham City Council Social Services Department (1996) *The Wraparound Project Final Report.* Birmingham City Council.

Blenkin, G and Yue, N. (1994) *'Profiling Early Years Practitioners: some first impressions from a national survey'.* Early Years 15, 1, 13-22.

Boyle, M (1976) 'The Great Divide', *Focus on Social Work and Service in Scotland,* 1976.

Braun, D (1990) *Shared Care at Hillfields Nursery Centre.* Community Education Development Centre, Coventry.

Bruce, T (1987) *Early Childhood Education.* Hodder and Stoughton.

Bruce, T (1991) *Time to Play in Early Childhood Education.* Hodder and Stoughton.

Central Advisory Council for Education (1967) *Children and their Primary Schools.* HMSO.

Department of Education and Science (1972) *Education: a Framework for Expansion.* HMSO.

Department of Education and Science (1990) *Starting with Quality: the report of the Committee of Inquiry into the quality of educational experience offered to three- and four-year-olds.* Chairman: Angela Rumbold. HMSO.

Department for Education and Employment/School Curriculum and Assessment Authority (1996) Desirable Outcomes for children's learning on entering compulsory education. DfEE.

Department of Health (1992) *The Health of the Nation: A Strategy for Health in England.* HMSO.

Department of Health and Social Security and Department of Education and Science (1976) *coordination of Services for Children Under Five*. DHSS

Department of Health and Social Security and Department of Education and Science (1978) *coordination of Services for Children Under Five*. DHSS

Duffy, B. and Griffin, S. (1994) *A Vision for Early Childhood Care and Education*. Early Childhood Education Forum.

Farrington, David: (1996). *Understanding and Preventing Youth Crime*. Joseph Rowntree Foundation.

Ferri, E, Birchall, D, Gingell, V, and Gipps, C (1981) *Combined Nursery Centres: a new approach to Education and Day Care*. National Children's Bureau.

Ford, R, (1996) *Childcare in the Balance*. Policy Studies Institute.

Gibbons, J, Conroy, S, and Bell, C (1995) *Operating the Child Protection System: A study of child protection practices in English Local Authorities*. HMSO.

Goldschmeid, E (1987) *Infants at Work*. Video available from the National Children's Bureau.

Goldschmeid, E (1994) *Heuristic Play with Objects*. Video available from the National Children's Bureau.

Goldschmeid, E and Jackson, S (1994) *People Under Three*. Routledge.

Holterman, S (1992) *Investing in Young Children: costing an education and day care service*. National Children's Bureau

Holterman, S. (1995) *Investing in Young Children: a reassessment of the cost of an education and day care service*. National Children's Bureau.

Independent on Sunday, November 24 1996, reporting figures compiled by the House of Commons library from official statistics.

Jarousse, J-P, Mingat, A, Richard, M and others, (1992) *La scolarisation maternelle à deux ans: effets pédagogiques et sociaux*. Education et Formation no.31.

Jenkins, S P and Jarvis, S (1996) *Changing Places: income mobility and policy dynamics in Britain*. Essex University ESRC Research Centre on Micro-social change.

Labour (1996) *Early Excellence: a head start for every child*. The Labour Party.

Moss, P and Penn, H (1996) *Transforming Nursery Education*. Paul Chapman.

Parsons, C (1996) *Exclusion from School: the Public Cost*. Commission for Racial Equality.

Perfect M, and Renshaw, J (1996) *Misspent Youth: Young People and Crime*. HMSO.

Pugh, G (1988) *Services for Under Fives: Developing a coordinated Approach*. National Children's Bureau.

Pugh, G, De'Ath, E and Smith, G (1994) *Confident parents: confident children: Policy and Practice in Parent Education and Support*. National Children's Bureau

Pugh, G and McQuail, S (1995) *Effective Organisation of Early Childhood Services*. National Children's Bureau.

Pugh, G (1996) *A vision for Early Childhood Services: Challenges and Opportunities*. Paper at a conference on the Future Shape of Early Years Services, National Children's Bureau.

Pugh, G (1996b) *Four-year-olds in school: what is appropriate provision?* Childfacts, Winter 1996. National Children's Bureau.

Pugh, G (ed). (1996c). *Education and Training in the Early Years*. National Children's Bureau.

Pugh, G and Owen, S (1996) *Evaluation of Nursery Vouchers: lessons from Phase I*. Interim report. National Children's Bureau.

Rutter, M (1985) 'Family and school influences on cognitive development.' *Journal of Child Psychology* 26 (5) 683-704.

Schweinhart L and Weikart, D (1993) *A summary of significant benefits: The High/Scope Perry pre school study through age 27*. Ypsilanti, Michigan: High/Scope UK.

Smith, M (1996) *Early Years Centres: A Paper on their background and development*. Paper for the ACC/AMA Early Years Task Force.

Statham J (1994) *Childcare in the Community: the provision of community-based, open access services for young children in family cantres*. Save the Children Fund.

Sylva, K (1994) 'The Impact of Early Learning on Children's Later Development' in *Start Right: the importance of early learning on children's later development*. Royal Society for the Encouragement of Arts, Manfacturers and Commerce.

Westminster City Council (1996) *Great Expectations*.

Whalley, M (1994) *Learning to be Strong: setting up a neighbourhood service for under fives and their families*. Hodder and Stoughton.

Whalley, M, Cowley, L and Whittaker, P (in press, due 1997). *Leadership and Management in the Early Years*. National Children's Bureau.

Williams, E (1996) 'More problems than solutions await Bradford's Mr Fixit,' *Times Educational Supplement*, October 25 1996.

Woodhead, M (1985) 'Pre-school education has long-term effects but can they be generalised?' *Oxford Review of Education 20, 2, 163-171*.

Index